AGE

—

The Unrecognised
Discrimination

AGE

The Unrecognised Discrimination

VIEWS
TO PROVOKE
A DEBATE

Editor:
Evelyn McEwen

© 1990, Age Concern England
1268 London Road
London SW16 4EJ

Editor: Claire Llewellyn
Design: David Warner
Production: Joyce O'Shaughnessy
Copy preparation: Vinnette Marshall

Typeset from disc by Impetus Graphics,
London SW17
Printed by Grosvenor Press, Portsmouth

ISBN 0-86242-094-6

Disclaimer
The views expressed in this book are those
of the authors and are not necessarily held
by the publishers.

CONTENTS

ACKNOWLEDGEMENTS

A considerable number of people have worked with me on the development of this book and my grateful thanks go to them all.

First and foremost I must acknowledge the co-operation and goodwill of the eight contributors. They have all displayed enormous enthusiasm for the project throughout and have borne my frequent queries and requests with unruffled patience.

My thanks are also due to Fred Baylis, John Gabriel, Dr Anne Roberts and Sally Robertson, all of whom read and commented on various parts of the text most instructively at draft stage.

In addition, I would like to thank Kate Callen, Jane Clarkson, Barbara Meredith, David Moncrieff, Ben Plowden and Sally West, all colleagues here at Age Concern, for their advice and encouragement during the prolonged editing process.

Finally, particular thanks are due to Claire Llewellyn for her invaluable assistance and support.

EVELYN McEWEN
May 1990

INTRODUCTION

A FORCE FOR CHANGE

It is an unfortunate fact that to be old is still equated far too often with far too many undesirable attributes, including dependency, rigidity of thought and the inability to learn new things. Factually such views are incorrect. The vast majority of today's older people are active, fit and independent. They have adapted to, and often been in the forefront of, more rapid and profound social, economic and technological changes than any previous generations. The personality traits which are frequently used to describe them in disparaging terms are to be found in some people at all ages and stages of life. They have nothing to do with the process of ageing in itself. Sadly, however, stereotyped views used by the young to describe those who are older tend to be adopted by people as they age and cause them to play out and conform to the role prescribed to them.

It is not surprising, therefore, that a combination of negative attitudes, stereotyped views and overt and covert practices, largely unrecognised as discriminatory, have resulted in many older people enduring narrowed horizons at a time when the potential for many fulfilling years has never been greater.

Age Concern England has a history of initiating wide discussion on issues of importance. This has demanded courage at times when difficult or contentious subjects have been made the subject of debate.

Age discrimination is one of these issues. Not only is it manifest at an institional level, it strikes home somewhere in each of us. The painful process of discovering it in aspects of our own personality, which we would rather were not exposed, is something that understandably we try to avoid.

For hundreds of years European society has reinforced and demonstrated its solidarity through blaming elderly witches and sorcerers for the ills which befell it. Brave young heroes and gentle, nubile maidens have triumphed over wicked ageing stepmothers, monstrous elderly abductors and whiskered and bearded despots.

Stereotypes tend to stick and to reinforce prejudice. Even those that are less negative are patronising in that they fit a vast number of people into a category that may bear no resemblance to the millions of individuals with an age range spanning thirty to forty years, who form our elderly population.

Incorrect assumptions about old people and the ageing process are also partly rooted in fear. As a society we are fearful of getting old – a justifiable feeling, given that for many it is a far from pleasant experience. But much of what is feared is not inevitable. It results from man-made situations that far too many people face as they grow old, when poverty is still a reality, choices are limited, opportunities for decision-making reduced and participation in the planning and design of services intended to improve the quality of their life still rare.

Those in the caring professions can be, usually quite unwittingly, 'ageist' in overprotecting elderly people, thereby diminishing their autonomy. This can easily lead to a denial of some of the rights that younger adults take for granted.

To deny people equal access to resources on the grounds of age is to marginalise them through discrimination. To consider them a burden on society is a likely result and adds to the diminution of their status and the value in which they are held. Then their age is seen to be the cause, rather than their problems the result, of the disadvantages so many people experience in later life.

The State pension in this country is set at a low level, so many people are still dependent on means tested benefits. They tend to be the very people whose long memories of the indignities of pre-war provision make them the group least likely to take up those benefits. Therefore, there are still a large number of older people whose lack of income is partly due to the fact that they do not claim what they are entitled to. The barriers which deter them from claiming their rights are an example of indirect discrimination.

Caricatured images of older people also diminish their status. The media tends not to feature older adults leading full lives and experiencing the entire gamut of emotions: love, pain and joy. The public equates all that is beautiful and active with youth. This stereotype means that when we are old we can no longer be any of these, so obviously most people do not want to become old. Many deny their own age as far as possible by distancing themselves from those who are already old, seeking to stay young. Through this denial they feel they retain the right to a lifestyle which old people are no longer entitled to enjoy.

Our current view of the purpose and value of education is biased, seeing it mainly as a preparation for work. Young people are an investment in the future; old people, by contrast, do not warrant educational resources as their working life is over and, in addition, they are considered incapable of learning new skills. Research over the years has clearly demonstrated this to be a fallacy, but the prejudice continues and spreads into the workplace, where age has systematically replaced ability as the factor determining the eligibility for a job.

When forced out of work through compulsory retirement, older people can then be blamed for failing to contribute to the economy. In such arguments the vast actual and potential contribution of the older generation is not taken into account, although several initiatives, such as Age Resource, are attempting to reverse this fact. The increasingly good health enjoyed by the majority of elderly people and the decreasing costs of maternity and child care are not set against the high costs of caring in a civilised and humane manner for the minority whose needs will continue to be a priority and require a high input of resources.

While the needs of the economy due to labour shortages and the increasing attractiveness of the older consumer market are beginning to change the negative perceptions widely held about older people, there are still far too many barriers facing those amongst this group seeking to make a contribution to society.

Therefore, there is no doubt that it is not an easy task that Age Concern has taken on in embarking on a concerted effort to fight age discrimination.

In such a process Age Concern England itself cannot be exempt from scrutiny and we need to question our own policies and practices with the aim of ensuring that our public statements are made from a standpoint of integrity. In 1988 in our capacity as the National Council on Ageing, the formal constitutional title of Age Concern England, through which we bring together over eighty national organisations in membership together with the Age Concern family of local organisations and the main representative bodies of older people in this country, we embarked on a major debate on ageism. This debate has challenged many people whose commitment to serving and working with the older sector of our population is indisputable, to look in depth at their own views and those of the organisations they represent. Discrimination is certainly not limited to the public and commercial domain, it exists in the voluntary sector. It is no easy task to eliminate this in our own organisations, but all of us need to be at the forefront of the changes we are seeking to bring about and not be satisfied with limited achievements.

As with racism and sexism, legal structures and procedures to combat ageism are essential. They provide the framework from which guidelines and benchmarks in good practice can be drawn. As with the other more readily acknowledged forms of discrimination, no-one can totally eliminate prejudiced views and thoughts in an entire population. It is possible, however, to stop those prejudices being translated into action and without legislation no-one has a cornerstone from which to argue that discriminatory action exists.

We are arguing strongly for a start to be made in this country through making upper age limits in recruitment advertising illegal and are bringing together a group of organisations to campaign vehemently to achieve this aim. We hope this will lead to judgements being made about people in paid work and in voluntary and public service on the basis of competence rather than on the number of birthdays they have celebrated.

From that point our aim will be to progress step-by-step into influencing change in the many other areas of life in which older people are subjected to the damaging effects of ageism, with harmful, degrading and often tragic results. Age Concern England is determined not to wait while this virulent form of discrimination – virtually endemic in our society – continues to harm the very people we as an organisation are here to serve. In concrete terms, we hope that the resolution to this effect to be brought forward by our Governing Body will in itself have a far-reaching effect in combating institutional ageism.

The views and arguments presented in the following chapters are not all necessarily those of Age Concern England, but the firm commitment to eliminate age discrimination certainly is. This book addresses a large number of aspects of life which are affected by ageism, but it is only a start. Readers will know about other ways in which discriminatory practice affects the lives of people as they age, blocking their potential for fulfilling lives and denying them the right to full self-determination. At Age Concern we are anxious to learn from other people's experience and we would, therefore, be very pleased to hear from anybody who knows of specific instances of age discrimination.

This book is only one contribution towards a task which is almost as great as the wider phenomenon of which it is a concomitant part, the ageing of society itself, the implications of which are so far-reaching as to warrant the dual title of the greatest triumph and the greatest challenge at the end of the 20th century.

I hope this book will convince its readers that age discrimination exists and help to bring the message to a much wider audience. Age Concern England will take action through continuing advocacy with persuasion and through educational programmes to eradicate this totally unacceptable feature of today's society.

SALLY GREENGROSS
Director
Age Concern England

1 AGEISM

THE FOUNDATION OF AGE DISCRIMINATION

STEVE SCRUTTON

Steve Scrutton is a social work manager in Northamptonshire. After a varied career in teaching, he became involved with older people while taking a postgraduate degree and training as a social worker. He believes that older people have had a raw deal, and through his writing he hopes to show where things have gone wrong and how more positive attitudes could be developed.

His first book *Counselling Older People* was published as part of the Age Concern Handbook series. His forthcoming one is to be about ageing and health.

My father died in 1979, aged 76. After a period of normal grieving, my mother, who was then 74, decided that she wanted to travel from Norwich to Northamptonshire to visit me, a journey of about 100 miles. Previously, she would have been driven by my father, but she announced that it was her intention to travel, alone, by train. My first reaction was that she was to do no such thing. I would go to Norwich and bring her myself. My second reaction was to let her do as she wished. After all, what were the reasons for not allowing her to travel alone? Indeed, she insisted on it, and did the entire trip by herself.

My initial reaction had been a prime, although mild, example of ageism in operation. My mother was quite capable of making the journey but, because of her age, I had felt that it would be wrong for me to allow her to undertake it. Such a decision, if carried through, would have been debilitating for my mother, who would have been made to feel dependent, no longer capable of making decisions for herself, or acting independently. Instead, she had not been a burden, either in my mind or, more importantly, in her own. She had demonstrated her independence and proven conclusively that her age was not a barrier.

This form of patronising ageism is common where there is genuine care for ageing people. We do not allow older people to work, because they are old. We protect older people from harm, real and imaginary, because we do not believe they can protect themselves. Our concern restricts their ability to fend for themselves. We clean their homes, fetch their shopping, ferry them to where they wish to go; and we do all this without thinking that our care might be undermining their independence, even their morale. We prevent them from taking risks, discourage them from taking physical exercise, and even deny their sexuality.[1] In many subtle ways our care demonstrates that we believe the ageing process makes independent action impossible. The reason we do so is entirely based on our perception of what older people should and should not be allowed to do for themselves – at their age.

There is another, more pernicious form of ageism. This is the ageism that arises from neglect, and from discounting the needs of older people. It is not based on compassion. Instead it deprives older people of social status and role, undermines their self-esteem, and denies them a fair share of social resources. Why else do we insist that older people cannot be employed after a certain age? Why else do we ensure that when they retire they receive subsistence-level pensions? Why else do we frequently talk of the 'demographic trends', implying that older people are a burden? Why else is the care of frail, dependent older people in hospitals and residential care so frequently a disgrace? And why else has the abuse of older people failed to become more of a social issue?

▬ What is ageism?

The attitudes which dominate any society usually reflect the interests of the most powerful and influential social groups. Such attitudes may not be shared by everyone, but are accepted by most people without question. Where the assumptions made about old age are negative they lead to ageism, which treats older people not as individuals but as a homogeneous group which can be discriminated against. Ageism creates and fosters prejudices about the nature and experience of old age. These usually project unpleasant images of older people which subtly undermine their personal value and worth. Commonly held ideas restrict the social role and status of older people, structure their expectations of themselves, prevent them achieving their potential and deny them equal opportunities.

Ageism, so defined, is broader than age discrimination. The reason for the discriminatory practices described throughout this book cannot be fully understood and tackled without reference to the concept of ageism.

▬ The social process of ageism

Each society defines and reacts to older people in ways which are often subtly, sometimes fundamentally, different from each other. The popularly held view of old age today is of very old people, usually women, living alone, socially isolated, managing on inadequate incomes, poorly housed, suffering ill health, dependent on younger carers, yet isolated from their families. Unhappy, withdrawn, but at the same time not interested in making new friends, they have lost their energy, enthusiasm and drive, and are no longer concerned with education or personal development. Their deteriorating physical and mental health offers only the prospect of further decline and the ultimate sentence of old age – death.

This depressing but widely held view of life in old age is the foundation upon which judgements are made about individual worth. It pervades the outlook and expectations of young and old alike, influencing their understanding and appreciation of the nature of old age. It forms the basis for contempt on the part of the young and strong for the old and weak, and the increasing fear of human mortality which old age seems to represent so vividly. Older people have absorbed these attitudes which they once held as young people, and lead their lives in ways which confirm the stereotyped images, and perpetuate the myths of ageism from generation to generation.

Racism, classism, disablism and sexism have developed through similar social processes. While they have much in common, ageism is perhaps different in two major respects. First, older people do not form an exclusive group, but one of which every individual will eventually become a member. The white racist will never be black; the male sexist will never be female; but the young ageist will grow old. Second, the discrimination which emanates from ageism can appear to result from the natural process of biological ageing rather than social creation. It is important to emphasise that the concept of ageism does not deny the ageing process, but rather seeks to distinguish between – on the one hand – ageing as a process of physiological decline and – on the other – the social phenomenon which forms the basis of the disadvantage and oppression of older people. Any consideration of ageism has to be clear about the difference.

■ The social creation of ageism

If different cultures, at different times, value older people in different ways, it indicates that our stereotypes are socially rather than biologically created. It is useful to confirm this in order to counter the popular idea that discrimination against older people arises entirely from the nature of old age.

Former civilisations have regarded and treated older people in very different ways. The historian, Minois[2], has delved systematically into the changing status of older people in history, and he has been able to link these changes to the dominant social ideas and circumstances of the time. In ancient Greece, the cult of youth and beauty, and the reverence for the elderly Homeric sage, created an ambivalence which has typified attitudes towards older people throughout history. In the Roman Empire, this ambivalence was demonstrated by the important role played by senior citizens, on the one hand, and their cruel subjection to the literary satire of the time on the other. In the Christian tradition, the image of the revered holy sage was contrasted with the condemnation of the ageing sinner.

Throughout history, two main factors have contributed to these historical fluctuations in the fortune of older people: physical strength, and the value placed on acquired knowledge and experience. Physical strength has always been highly regarded. The theory of the 'survival of the fittest' predicts that the old and weak must eventually succumb to the young and strong, and that this is necessary for the future vitality of the species. Social life based on this condition can hardly be favourable to older people, and the more turbulent and anarchical the times, the worse their condition and status has been. It is the loss of strength associated with old age that has permitted and continues to permit the abuse of older people.

The respect once given to older people for their knowledge and experience has suffered as a result of several factors: the decline of custom, the acceleration of change and the loss of oral traditions. Civilisations which pass on their learning and experience verbally have to rely on older citizens to provide the vital link between generations. The development of writing and the widespread circulation of books undermined the importance of memory, thereby destroying one of the most useful social functions provided by older people.

For these reasons, prejudice against age is certainly not new. Aristotle (384-322 BC), in his *Rhetoric,* accused older people of every conceivable fault. He described them as cowardly, hesitant, selfish, timorous, suspicious, fearful, parsimonious, miserly, small-minded, ill-humoured and avaricious. This form of ageism has probably always existed. It is unlikely that there has ever been a golden age, in which elders have been respected solely for their age. There has always been a close correlation between the status of older people, and their personal achievement. The greater the past achievement and the higher the social class, the more status individuals have been able to maintain in old age. Among the poor the situation has always been more difficult. When older people were no longer able to fend for themselves, they became a burden of no further value, and often ended their lives despised and in extreme poverty.

Despite these disadvantages, many older people have been able to maintain their social status by remaining active, alert and healthy. The ability to maintain physical and mental powers has allowed some individuals to pursue their chosen careers regardless of their age. They are the exceptions that prove the rule, 'the rule' being the dominant expectations of the time. The evidence of Western civilisation suggests that the status of older people has been generally low, but variably so. While it was low in ancient Greece, it was higher in the Hellenistic world. Similarly, it was higher during the early centuries of the Roman republic than in the later Empire period, and while it was low during the turbulence of the early Middle Ages, it reached a peak in the fourteenth and fifteenth centuries, when the importance of older people was enhanced by their ability to survive the plagues of the era.[2]

Thus, although capitalism is blamed by many workers for the treatment older people receive today, it is clear that ageism has a history which long predates this form of social organisation. However, the human disruption caused by the agricultural and industrial revolutions did produce in the West a social environment which was particularly unfavourable to older people. If they were unable to take part in hard productive work, they became surplus to the manpower requirements of the new industrial society. This led to two main developments. Initially, older people were removed from the community supports which traditionally looked after them and subjected to the rigours of a 'work or starve' philosophy. Subsequently, nineteenth-century philanthropy sought to protect older people from the worst impacts of the economic climate, and such efforts culminated in the introduction of pension legislation. Unfortunately, through fixed ages for the receipt of pensions, these reforms also forcibly prevented older people being productive members of the society and thereby reduced their social status.

Longevity was once a rarer phenomenon than it is in the late twentieth century. As such, it evoked curiosity and some awe. In a time when birthrates are decreasing in many countries, it creates fear. In Britain where there has been a continuing decline in the birthrate this century, politicians who talk about the 'burden' of old age reveal their concern that a smaller working population will be forced to support a growing number of retired people. This number will grow dramatically as the baby boom generation reaches retirement in the twenty-first century (see table opposite).

In the next 30 years, Britain expects the number of people over 65 to increase by 20% and the number of people over 84 to increase by 47%. This prospect has led to a retrenchment in state pension provision and an emphasis on informal caring systems, two attempts to reduce the need for society to foot the bill of its ageing population.

The elderly population in Great Britain: past, present and future[3]

	65+	%	75+	%	85+	%
1901	1734	4.7	507	1.4	57	0.15
1931	3316	7.4	902	2.1	108	0.24
1951	5332	10.9	1731	3.5	218	0.45
1961	6046	11.8	2167	4.2	329	0.64
1971	7140	13.2	2536	4.7	462	0.86
1981	7985	15.0	3053	5.7	552	1.03

Projections for the future (made in 1987)

	65+	%	75+	%	85+	%
1987	8624	15.6	3699	6.7	746	1.3
1991	8838	15.8	3925	7.0	875	1.6
2001	8984	15.6	4309	7.5	1144	2.0
2011	9425	16.1	4372	7.5	1291	2.2
2021	10642	18.0	4699	7.9	1287	2.2
2027	11472	19.2	5308	8.9	1326	2.2

In the first column of figures, the size of the population is given *in thousands*.
In the second column, the number is expressed as a percentage of the total population of
the country.

The status of older people is also dependent on the social context in which people live, and this is made apparent by the wide variation in ageing patterns in different ethnic, geographic and socio-economic sub-cultures.[4] In some cultures, older people are deprived of esteem, suffer severe neglect and, in extreme cases, the frail and weak are simply left to die.

Far Eastern cultures appear to be the most favourable in which to grow old. Elders are widely respected and have high social status. Yet even here deference for old age is not universal or unconditional but is based upon personal achievements or the special knowledge and skills that the individual can offer. Moreover, when these societies become industrialised and urbanised another set of values begins to undermine these time-honoured traditions. The respect for elders in Japan is gradually waning as a result.

A similar weakening of traditional cultural values can be witnessed in Britain, where Asian communities have now been subjected to dominant Western values for several generations. There has developed what has been described as a 'transition trap', experienced by the generation which has cared for their elders in the traditional manner, but whose children have increasingly embraced Western lifestyles, and fail to fulfil customary expectations about caring for their parents.

This pattern of cultural change is one of the clearest indications of the powerful impact that dominant social attitudes and values have on the status and treatment of older people. Both historical and cultural comparisons indicate that the ideas we have about old age are *as* important, probably *more* important than biological ageing in determining the way old age is perceived, and how older people are treated. Where the status of older people is low, it is because these attitudes determine that it will be low, not because it is a natural consequence of the ageing process. This raises the important question of where our ageism originates.

Ageism and the process of socialisation

From birth onwards we are all presented with unflattering images of old age. There has never been a time more conscious of chronological age than our own. Life is presented as a succession of 'ages': from birth, through babyhood, infancy, childhood, adolescence, adulthood, middle age and finally old age. Youth represents potential for future growth and development, a time of hope and expectation. Thereafter all is decline, with an increasing if unspoken fear of ageing. It is this process of socialisation — the gradual adoption of values and norms associated with social roles — which generates ageism. Infants do not discriminate on the basis of age. Their judgement of people is based entirely on whether they are treated gently or harshly, kindly or unkindly, with love or with disdain. It is socialisation that transforms ageing into something that is to be feared, and leads us to believe that older people are to be pitied.

Many school textbooks, from the earliest readers, portray older people as clumsy, frail, pathetic, and needing to be helped across roads, while younger members of the family are happily enjoying an exciting and glamorous life. Many pre-school poetry collections include material which presents negative images of older people.[5] These early influences are probably the first to make an impression on the minds of young children, and this impression is confirmed in later school years, not least in classic literature. In Shakespeare's *As You Like It*, for example, the melancholy Jacques describes old age as:

'. . . second childishness and mere oblivion,

Sans teeth, sans eyes, sans taste, sans everything.'[6]

Our education system also subtly confirms the ageist idea that older people are not educable and are not interested in personal development. The very foundation of our modern system, the 1944 Education Act, discusses the education of 'the people' but effectively means the education of those between 5 and 16 years. Adults have no statutory rights to education and, as one educational gerontologist writes, 'if adult education is marginalised then the education of older adults is marginalised to the margins of the margin.'[7]

Language is another powerful method of structuring attitudes about old age. In this area our language is highly expressive and almost invariably derogatory, infantilising or pitying. Words and phrases in common usage, such as 'mutton dressed as lamb', 'dirty old man', 'silly old woman', 'old fogies', 'old ducks', 'old biddy', 'old codger', 'old dears' and 'old folk' all conjure up images which leave little doubt about the nature and experience of old age.

Nor is the impact confined to popular expressions. *Roget's Thesaurus*, a classic English text which seeks to arrange words 'according to the ideas which they express', describes old age by such nouns as 'senility, grey hairs, climacteric, declining years, decrepitude, hoary age, caducity, superannuation, second childhood, dotage, decline of life' and, even more graphically, by the adjectives 'senile, run to seed, declining, waning, past one's prime, grey, hoary, venerable, time-worn, antiquated, doddering, decrepit, superannuated, stricken in years, wrinkled, having one foot in the grave.'

The assumption that old people are rigid, less capable, less willing to adapt to new developments, and unable to change is firmly rooted in modern psychological theory. The father of modern psychology, Sigmund Freud believed '. . . psychiatry is not possible near or above the age of 50; the elasticity of the mental processes on which the treatment depends is as a rule lacking – old people are not educable.'[8]

This view has had an influential impact on psychology, and although some might now consider such ideas outmoded, they continue to have an enduring effect on public perceptions of old age. The association between age, adaptability, and psychological theory remains one of the major factors that disables older people, particularly within a society in which 'change' and 'progress' are increasingly important.

Ageism is also firmly rooted in our pervasively influential religious beliefs. Many religions encourage the idea that our current condition is temporary, and that old age should be a time of looking towards our place in the next life which is more important. Suffering is part of our preparation for the hereafter. Death, our link to a better world, is to be welcomed rather than feared. Happiness and fulfilment will be abundantly available in heaven, valhalla, or nirvana.

The impact of religious belief on the attitudes to life of older people is particularly strong. These attitudes in Christian tradition can be traced back to ideas which linked old men with the image of sin, and old age as a curse and a punishment.[9] In Western tradition, the belief that a normal lifespan was the biblical 'three score years and ten' has shaped the expectations of older people, and justified a lack of social provision.

Medical opinion is another influential source of dominant social attitudes, and its views on ageing are central to the expectations we have about the 'normal' condition of older people. A common image of health in old age is one associated with the loss of energy and personal drive, significantly greater need for rest, long and increasing periods of sickness, permanent experience of pain and discomfort, increasing immobility, the gradual loss of personal control and responsibility, the onset of incontinence, with the resulting loss of dignity and self-respect, increasing confusion, and ultimately the most feared condition of all, senility.

The image of old age as a time of pain, illness and disease has often implied that older people actually owe their continuing existence to medical expertise alone. Unfortunately, comments made by some doctors to older people nurture and encourage the view that pain, illness and disease are an unavoidable feature of normal ageing. The biological assumptions involved in such statements are based on a series of half-truths about the ageing process, extended so that they appear to support explanations about the nature of life and health in old age that are not justified by the facts. For instance, while brain cells do die and are not replaced, their loss is not an explanation for senility. Yet through such biological 'explanations', dementia is perceived as part of the normal, natural process of ageing. Moreover, once this premise is accepted there is less reason to seek to cure it; pain, illness and disease become an accepted consequence of old age.

The association between youth and beauty has been evident throughout history, particularly in ancient Greece and during the Renaissance. It is equally apparent today when many people go to considerable lengths to maintain the appearance of youthfulness by the use of vitamins, beauty preparations of all descriptions, hormone treatment, plastic surgery and much else besides. The link that is assumed between beauty and youth implies a link between old age and ugliness, and is detrimental to older people. It supports the belief that ageing makes people unattractive, and no longer physically or sexually interesting. The impact on older women is greater than for older men, as dominant sexist ideas have created the belief that being attractive is more important for women.

Consequently, dual standards are applied. Eyebrows are raised considerably higher by the idea of an older woman with her 'toy boy' than an older man with a much younger girlfriend.

■ Structural ageism

The most pernicious aspect of ageism is not that which is present in the minds and attitudes of individuals, but that which is confirmed and reinforced by the functions and rules of everyday social life. The structural analysis of ageing has become increasingly prominent in recent years.[10] The close association between productivity and social status within the 'work cultures' of Western capitalist societies has been well documented. Marx believed that capitalist values were completely determined by considerations of productivity. Weber saw capitalism as characterised by an emphasis on work and activity and highlighted the effect this had on the moral as well as the economic and political development of a society. Durkheim recognised this too when he defined the 'division of labour' as a system of moral integration as well as economic production.

This analysis has had important implications for older people. Compulsory retirement enforces non-productivity, depresses social status, and promotes the idea of old people as a burden. It is the basis for age discrimination through neglect. Medical, educational and social service provision becomes a low priority if it is considered that there is only a marginal return on such investment. The result is that ageism is at its most vicious when older people compete for limited resources, for they are often denied equal access – solely by virtue of their age.

The structural confirmation of ageism is vitally significant. If age discrimination was entirely a matter of individual attitudes it could be more easily tackled. It is when ageist attitudes become part of the rules of institutions, govern the conduct of social life, and blend imperceptibly into everyday values and attitudes that they have a drastic effect on the way older people lead their lives. Descriptions of how this is done are found in subsequent chapters. Their combined conclusion is a dramatic one. Older people, on the basis of chronological age, are progressively removed from economic life, which provides them not only with income, but structures their daily routines and integrates them into regular social relationships. Compulsory retirement places older people in a no-win situation; they are not allowed to work in order to earn their living; nevertheless, their enforced lack of productivity makes them a 'burden', and serves to devalue them.

The most immediate effect of retirement is a dramatic reduction in living standards. Our welfare state encourages, even ensures, poverty among retired people. State pensions have remained fixed at subsistence levels. Non-means-tested welfare benefits display many features of structural ageism. The maximum social security payments for older people living in residential care homes are lower than for younger, physically handicapped people. Other disablement benefits cannot be claimed once an individual has reached pensionable age, implying that disability is a normal part of old age. The perception that disability is age-related ultimately influences the take-up rate of these benefits, for many older frail people fail to claim allowances to which they are entitled because they assume that their problems result from old age rather than disability.[11]

The structural neglect of older people reaches its peak when they become frail or dependent. Ageist attitudes ensure that caring for dependent and vulnerable older people is regarded as a low prestige, low priority enterprise by both health professionals and social workers. The low standards of residential care have been a topic of concern for many years. There have been a number of major scandals, the most significant being the Nye Bevan Lodge investigation in 1988, in which residents were found to have been illegally deprived of their money, made to queue naked for baths, and subjected to other practices which included physical and sexual assault. It was widely recognised at the time that these practices were the tip of a much larger iceberg of old-age abuse.

I was personally involved in the investigation of a private residential home for older people in Northampton, in which gross practices against residents were uncovered. Neither of these events, nor other similar ones, have hit the imagination of the media or the public with the same force as the similar serious scandals involving children.[12]

Weaker members of society are always vulnerable to mistreatment. Abuse of children has been recognised as an important concern because children are seen to represent the future; to abuse them is to abuse the future welfare of the nation. Child protection has therefore been given priority status, resulting in a plethora of legislation, directives, regulations and procedures, all adopted to protect the well-being of children.

The abuse of older people has not attained equal priority. The Northampton investigation centred on an elderly woman, suffering dementia, who was found to have a double fracture of the jaw. There was no acceptable explanation for the injuries, and the injuries were consistent with a single blow. Yet the medical authorities would not clearly state this, nor did the police believe that they had a case capable of being taken further, not least because the abused woman could not tell us how it had happened. While I was personally convinced that abuse had taken place, it appeared that no further action was likely.

The contrast between this inactivity and the action which would have been taken had the injured individual been a young child, was a stark one. There would have been more medical concern. The social services would have had powers to protect not only the injured party (even without evidence that could be proven in court), but also all the other children, probably by their removal from the home. Public concern, legislation, departmental procedures, and pressure on professional staff would have combined to ensure that effective action was taken. In contrast, lack of public concern, the absence of legislation and departmental procedures, and a general lack of professional concern seemed to conspire in the opposite direction with regard to this elderly woman. In his survey, the social worker Mervyn Eastman states that 'society does not even accept that old-age abuse takes place, let alone appreciate the reasons why it happens.'[13] His view seems to be undeniable in this situation, and it serves to convince me that ageism will never be tackled unless recognition of the problem is followed by the introduction of positive measures.

Yet, Eastman's statement leads to another vital question that needs to be addressed. Why is it that structural ageism sanctions discrimination against older people and enables it to continue unnoticed on a daily basis, and remain unchanged over many years? Further, how can this situation occur in a society which would consider itself to be both civilised and compassionate in its dealings with older people?

▬ The denial of ageism and the myth of philanthropy

Despite the widespread ageism which exists at both the individual and structural level, there remains widespread social ignorance and denial of its impact. The result is that the evidence for ageism remains unaltered, and the assumptions upon which ageism is based are preserved and perpetuated.

In its place has developed the myth of philanthropy. This is based upon the belief that older people are treated with greater compassion now than ever before. To confirm this, more comfortable images of old people have been created, enabling us to believe that older people are leading lives which are happy, contented and fulfilled. These are images of older people as kindly and inoffensive, sitting in front of their fires, or enjoying winter in hotels on the Costa del Sol. When they do need support, there is the comforting notion that the welfare state and National Health Service are looking after their needs better than ever before.

The denial of ageism can go further, with older people often being blamed for their own situation. Many professional people, including some gerontologists, consistently emphasise physical, psychological and social decline above all other factors in the characteristics and capacities of older people.[14] In doing so, they reveal how accustomed they have become to working with entrenched and unquestioned assumptions that such loss and decline is caused by age alone. We have even constructed elaborate theories to make us feel better about the lives older people lead. The theory of disengagement[15] has led us to believe that it is a normal feature of growing old to withdraw from social life, that isolation and loneliness is a chosen path and not the product of enforced retirement, low income, low status and inadequate social provision. The result is a tendency to 'blame the victim', a belief that older people have caused the plight in which they find themselves.

More convincing is the idea of 'structured dependence'[16], which suggests that dependency in old age is more usually a social than a biological or individual creation. The idea is graphically summarised by Alison Norman: 'We are all familiar with the advertisements and Christmas begging letters which ask for money in terms which suggest that old people are in danger of hypothermia or social isolation simply because they are old – not because they do not have sufficient incomes to heat and repair their homes or to pay for a taxi or telephone.'[17]

The situation of older people from ethnic-minority communities can be worse. The assumption that they are not neglected, and that cultural values ensure they will be cared for adequately, has been challenged by Norman.[18] Her concept of 'triple jeopardy' demonstrates that elders from such groups suffer from dominant Western social values in three distinct ways: psychologically, bureaucratically and financially.

The myth of philanthropy is quickly discredited by a realistic look at how older people lead their lives. However, the myth is constantly perpetuated in subtle ways; for instance, through apparently 'charitable' views of old age. In responses to a recent questionnaire from members of Age Concern England's governing body,[19] it was notable that few saw concessionary entitlement to services as discriminatory and patronising, only necessary in a society which implicitly recognises that older people are not treated fairly. The special treatment that concessions represent removes from older people the dignity associated with being able to function independently without the need for subsidy or support.

All forms of charity can have the same unfortunate, unintentional impact. The value of charity is twofold: it is aimed at helping the recipient, but it is also beneficial to the giver. Charity salves our conscience, allows us to feel that something is being done, that what is being done is sufficient, and that we have played our part in doing it. This is an integral part of the denial of ageism. We have old age pensions; but they are not sufficient. We have a National Health Service; but it does not deal adequately with the illnesses of old age.

In similar vein, dare it be said that the charitable function of Age Concern serves this dual function? To what extent does its dependence on charitable donations make it an involuntary party in the game of denial? If it were more forcefully to challenge the ageism that underlies the social structure, would it be in danger of provoking a backlash from those of its supporters who do not wish to be reminded that all is not well, despite their charity? Is Age Concern contributing to the idea that something effective is being done? Does it address the issue that it is the impact of social structures on older people that needs to be challenged, and that any amount of charitable good work is not going to fundamentally alter this situation? Is it strident enough in stating that not enough is being achieved? Despite its undoubted contribution in the past 50 years, perhaps these are questions that it needs to address now it is embarking on the journey to its centenary.

The consequence of the widespread denial of ageism is a strong social taboo surrounding the subject of old age, decline and death. Simone de Beauvoir asserted that 'society looks upon old age as a kind of shameful secret that it is unseemly to mention'.[20] Young people frequently dismiss remarks which older people may make about their impending or eventual death. Such thoughts are usually considered to be unnecessarily morbid, although the subject is probably more painful for younger people than those who more closely and personally face their own decline and death. For many older people this taboo is unhelpful and leads to difficulties, including an inability to prepare for and come to terms with the realities of old age, with physical and mental decline, and ultimately with death itself.[21]

Countering ageism
Ageism surrounds us, but it passes largely unnoticed and unchallenged. Moreover, just like racism and sexism, it is so engrained within the structure of social life that it is unlikely to be challenged effectively by rational argument or

appeals to the more philanthropic side of human nature.

There are a number of general strategies which are useful in combating ageism. Increased awareness is the basis on which they can be developed. Only when we are more aware of our personal attitudes can we become active in confronting ageism wherever it is encountered. Mary Marshall explores and develops this vital question in the next chapter.

Ageism-awareness campaigns and anti-ageist strategies, while essential, are not sufficient to bring about the level of change which is required. Age discrimination is so intertwined with the social fabric that legal action must become the major objective. There are no statutory safeguards against ageist practices, no equivalent of the Race Relations Act or Equal Opportunities legislation. Legislation will not end ageism, but it will bring the issues into sharper focus and force a re-appraisal of current social practices. There are several areas in which legal protection is required. The first of these is in the field of employment. Legislation is needed to protect the right to employment of older people by outlawing discriminatory practices in advertising and filling job vacancies. Individuals should also have the right to choose their own time of retirement. The second area requiring legislation is where older people have been discriminated against to such an extent that they have been put in jeopardy. Legal safeguards are necessary to protect their money and property and a way should be found to provide security of tenure for dependent older people in residential care. There should also be legislation which will protect older people against bad practice and abuse in both private and public residential care and nursing homes and in hospitals.

These defensive and protective proposals could be reinforced by a single measure, brilliant in its simplicity, which would guard against old-age discrimination more effectively than any other. This would be to outlaw general references to age in all current and future legislation where it is used to imply frailty or the need for services. Such a measure would have a dramatic impact. For example, the right to work would depend solely upon individual ability to do the job; the renewal of an annual driving licence after the age of 70 would have to be replaced by measures which are not triggered simply by people reaching a certain age.

The use of the word 'age' in legislation has helped to create age discrimination. Age was put alongside grave chronic disease, infirmity or physical incapacity as a qualifier in the 1948 National Assistance Act, and to this day the word continues to be used in legislation as a blanket term to imply dependence.

This practice encourages the belief that old age is a condition similar to disability. To ban the use of the word in legislation would encourage the awareness that age is not an illness or a disability. It would encourage the idea that to be old and disabled is not so different from being young and disabled; that dementia is a mental *illness*, not an inevitable feature of old age. It would stress that it is the circumstances and condition of individuals, not their age, that is significant.

Such a move would force a re-appraisal of ageist assumptions and encourage more positive attitudes which judge individual ability according to performance rather than chronological age. Pessimism about the nature of old age is perhaps the greatest enemy of a happy and fulfilled old age. To develop more positive images of ageing in this way is not a contrived attempt to pursue attitudes which are unreal, but an effort to seek redress to the current imbalance created by ageism. The starting point is to accept that each individual develops and evolves throughout life, and that the final stages of life are as important as any other. As Gore has said: 'Life lived as a continuum, is a garnering and enriching experience. It becomes a process of addition rather than subtraction; of a growing maturity rather than a loss of youth, of evolution rather than dissolution. It removes the pernicious, if subconscious obsession with calendar age, which precludes some of us from learning new things, or undertaking new tasks, or taking a new interest in the world around us.'[22] Legislative change would bring about a positive re-assessment of the social role of older people. It would help to create a more responsive social climate, enabling them to fulfil their potential and conclude their lives with dignity.

Moreover, legislation could galvanise the power of older people, countering the ageist idea that they cannot represent their own interests. The 'Grey' movement, in the shape of organised pensioners' groups, is becoming stronger. I hope they will challenge the images which restrain and persecute older people at present, and seek to shift public attitudes about the nature of old age. Collectively, older people need to exploit the full potential of their influence, which will only increase as their numbers grow, in order both to maintain responsibility for their own lives, and to demand their full social, political and economic rights.

2 PROUD TO BE OLD

ATTITUDES TO AGE AND AGEING

MARY MARSHALL

Mary Marshall is the Director of the Dementia Services Development Centre at Stirling University. She has enjoyed working with older people for nearly 20 years as a social worker, a researcher and most recently as

Director of Age Concern Scotland. She is 44 and believes that we have to learn to talk about our own ageing if we are to effectively link personal and social change.

The vision of Mrs Thatcher raising her arms at the Tory Party Conference and saying she is 'proud to be old' is so unlikely that it makes us smile. And yet by most definitions she is old. She is past the normal age at which women retire and she is entitled to a railcard. She is a grandmother. We have to ask ourselves why Mrs Thatcher would never say she was proud to be old. Why is the word 'old' so distasteful? Why do people use the word as an insult? Why do older people not see themselves as old? Discrimination is legitimised by negative attitudes and assumptions, and that is why these need to be examined and confronted.

In a Gallup Poll survey conducted for Sidhartha Films Ltd[1] of nearly 1000 people aged over 60, 78 per cent agreed with the statement 'I never think of myself as old', and only 14 per cent disagreed. If you ask old people whether they ever think of themselves as old, they tell you it is only when they are ill or feeling very unhappy. From the age of about 40, people are increasingly ashamed of their ageing. It is socially very inept to ask someone their age and, if they tell you, it is often in an embarrassed whisper. I have seen people close to tears as they own up to being over 50. Very few people share the view expressed in *Time* magazine that 'Ageing has become very stylish. All the best people are doing it.'[2]

Yet increasing numbers of people in Britain *are* old: more than ten million are over retirement age today. As part of the post-war baby bulge, I am confidently expecting to spend at least 20 years in retirement along with an unprecedented number of my peers. I intend to have a thoroughly enjoyable and lengthy period without paid work. These expectations are quite remarkable. The phenomenon of the bulk of the population surviving infancy and living well into their 70s and 80s is quite new and something to be proud of. Negative attitudes to ageing may, in part, be the result of the time lag between social change and a change in people's attitudes.

Attitudes are a way of making sense of the world, of organising what we see and what we experience. Clearly linked to language and concepts which we can put into words, attitudes are usually held collectively. That is to say that our attitudes are strongly influenced by others: people we mix with, television and radio, papers, magazines and books. Putting our experiences and views into words gives them meaning and enables us to feel confident and in control. Marris[3] and Parkes[4] are both sociologists who have studied bereavement and loss. They consider that you can only move on from an unhappy experience if you have given it some meaning. Marris suggests that this personal experience can also be a social phenomenon: families and communities have to give meaning to events to cope with them. But, of course, having a system of beliefs or attitudes also conditions the way we look at the world; what we actually see. It becomes impossible to say which comes first: the attitudes we hold or what we experience. On a grander scale this is the perennial argument about whether ideologies follow social changes or create them. It must be an interplay between the two and will vary in different circumstances.

One of the major changes to which our society must give meaning is the increasing number of people over the age of retirement, especially those in their 80s and 90s. There are always two tasks for professionals involved in social change: to change society for the better and to change attitudes. The task of this chapter is to look at attitudes to ageing and old people, to look at their consequences and to consider changing them. Social circumstances and social change is the task of the rest of this book.

▬ Negative attitudes

Many people writing about negative attitudes towards old age suggest that such attitudes are widely held and refer to most old people. One health visitor, for example, says that: 'Society finds it easy to decide when people are old. Women are old when they reach 60 and men are old at 65. Then they can join the ranks of the OAPs, the poor and powerless.' She continues: 'Ageism... is a prejudice which enables us all, young and old to consider old people as useless, incontinent, senile, asexual and immobile.'[5] This passionate article was written in 1985, and the rapidity of social change and changes in attitude since then, already make some qualification necessary. Although these negative attitudes remain, they are directed more at some groups than others.

There is a greater recognition than there was five years ago that the ten million people over retirement age are not homogeneous. Indeed, they are much less alike than any other group of people whose ages span 40 years, because we all become less alike as we grow older. We all develop throughout our lives, but experiences affect and change us differently. There is often a legitimate but hazy division into two 'groups'of older people: the young, recently retired and the older group. Obviously, however, these two groups differ according to your viewpoint; for example, on the basis of the extent of poor physical and mental health, on the proportions of men and women, on the extent of poverty and poor housing and the numbers living alone. There is no clear line between one group and another, and the differences are only relative.

There is a clearly perceptible change of attitude by the public and the people themselves to the relatively affluent and healthy newly retired: the Jollies (Jet-Setting Oldies with Lots of Loot) and the Woopies (Well-Off Older People). These fortunate people are able to seize the opportunities of more leisure time. They have also attracted their own market in terms of housing, holidays, magazines, insurance and even a whole weekend supplement of the *Financial Times* (6 January 1990). They are thus highly visible. They are the 'stylish ageing', but they are not a majority. Many of their peers are much less visible because they are carers trapped at home or are struggling to make ends meet.

In spite of their being only a minority of the pensioner population, affluent, active, newly retired people are slowly changing public attitudes. They are not seen as 'old'. Increasingly, negative attitudes are towards older, frailer people, who are now the main victims of ageism. A study published by Age Concern Scotland concluded: 'Ageism leads to a perception of old age as an affliction or disease which turns us into a special kind of being which is not fully human.'[6]

Another change in recent years is that most people have become aware of the term 'ageism', but there is still little effort to understand its causes and consequences.

The media

The media are crucially important in any contemporary discussion of attitudes. As a BBC resource pack states, 'the media, in the way they portray older people, tend to mirror society's beliefs about old age.'[7]

Attitudes in the media are slowly changing, but we are still presented with stereotyped images of older people. It is encouraging that the National Union of Journalists has now inserted an anti-ageist clause into its code of conduct. Most of us, however, are aware that tabloid newspapers still talk patronisingly about 'old folk', but the ageism of serious journals and newspapers is not always recognised.

Respondents to a questionnaire on age discrimination from members of Age Concern England's governing body highlighted this point. They felt that the press laid too great an emphasis on the frailty of older people and situations where they were in danger, rather than showing them as active members of the community. Anyone over 60, they thought, was labelled 'aged'.[8] Moreover, older people are often treated as if they were not adult, and are patronised by journalists who ask questions like: 'How do you put your grandmother in a home?'

The authors of the BBC resource pack identify the influential role played by television in the debate. Indeed, they conclude that 'it is television that gives millions of people their basic idea of reality', and this may be particularly true for older people, who on average watch 33 hours of television a week, 11 hours more than the national average. While special programmes for older viewers undoubtedly offer information and support, television companies may use them as an excuse for not including realistic portrayals of older people in their mainstream peak-time programmes. For example, many soap operas omit older people entirely, as if we were all perpetually middle-aged! Elsewhere, particularly in sitcoms, older people are crudely portrayed as being either enfeebled, vague and forgetful or, at the other extreme, cantankerous battleaxes.

On the news and in documentaries, as in the press, there is a concentration of stories about attacks on elderly people or abuse in old people's homes, which inevitably reinforces fear about old age. These are all editorial choices, and few of them create positive images for television audiences.

Until we have older people formulating policy, producing documentaries, reading the news and fronting arts and cultural programmes, we will not have removed ageism from television. Well-respected older male broadcasters like David Jacobs and Robert Dougall may continue to get the opportunity to host programmes aimed particularly at older people, but they will no longer present mainstream programmes. Older women will continue to disappear from public view altogether.

In any discusssion about the influence of the media over our perception of reality, it is important to recognise that millions of people form an idea of reality which is based firmly on experience, not on media images, and that these millions include most older people. Nevertheless, the media – particularly television – has enormous power; they can undoubtedly reinforce or fail to challenge attitudes in us all.

The formation of attitudes

Alison Norman in her challenging discussion paper suggests very basic origins for ageism: 'We have, after all, an animal inheritance and it is animal instinct to challenge and destroy the leader of the herd when his strength begins to fail and to abandon to their fate animals which are too weak to keep up with the rest.'[9] The question is how strong these instincts are in us. If we consider them stronger than the instinct to value the wisdom of old age or the instinct to care for those less able than ourselves, then we have to concede that the battle against ageism is a very hard one. Our attitudes are profoundly influenced by our own experiences both in the past and in the present. Our childhood experiences are very important. The wicked old women of fairy stories are a shared memory. More important are our relationships with older people like grandparents, or great-grandparents now that four-generation families are increasingly common. Some children are abused by grandparents, or terrorised by them; others are neglected by their parents because their grandparents are so demanding. On the other hand, many children have very close and loving relationships with their grandparents or other special old people who give them time and affection. The National Council for the Aged in the Republic of Ireland reports that in a sample of schoolchildren 62 per cent felt they had a friendly relationship with older people in general. Sadly, over half of the sample experienced some fear or anxiety about growing old themselves.[10]

This fear and anxiety about ageing and our future elderly selves is probably common to us all. As a character in Doris Lessing's novel *The Diaries of Jane Somers*, says about old people, 'I had not seen them. That was because I was afraid of being like them.'[11] Olive Stevenson[12] points out how difficult it is to empathise with older people because we have not had the same experiences. Death, for example, is part of old age; not just one's own approaching death, but the death of one's friends and family. Most people dread the possibility of dementia; many believe it is inevitable. Most people dread dependence and have no understanding of the very limited extent of total dependence in old age. But, in a sense, all of life is about learning to cope with old age. Every experience we have should make us better able to cope in the future. The accumulation of life's experience should make us at our wisest when we are old.

The extent to which life is difficult in old age is by no means all determined by nature. Poverty, poor housing, second rate services and negative personal interactions are common. When we look at older people we often see large groups of grey heads on coaches or in cheap supermarkets. We fail to make the connection that this may be a consequence of low income. Poor health itself, so much associated with old age, is affected by lack of money for nourishing food, warm houses and holidays.

Fear and anxiety, then, may have a sound basis. What is wrong is the tendency to generalise negative attitudes and to blame the victim. Because many old people are poor, or mentally or physically frail, it is assumed that they are also rigid, unable to learn, unable to make new relationships, and so on. It is also assumed that these qualities are true of most old people. Many of these assumptions are based on ignorance.

Blaming the victim is a characteristic of any prejudice. The fact that women are less successful than men and are often financially dependent on them is attributed to their being less able. Similarly, old people are seen in the same light, which explains their lack of employment or active leisure pursuits. These overwhelmingly negative attitudes prevent many people from seeing more than a grey head. What you do not expect to find, you seldom do find.

■ Older people themselves

As we reach old age, these negative attitudes will still be with us. Many old people, especially in the older age groups, have very low expectations and feel undeserving. Some of this must be because they are a generation that 'made shift' through the wars and the depression. Some of it is about coming to terms with reality. There is no point in raging against your circumstances if you are powerless to do anything about them. The power that older people might have collectively through the ballot box is not exercised. *Polls Apart?* a study of voting patterns conducted by the Centre for Policy on Ageing, found that older people do not vote on the basis of self-interest (eg pensions); they vote on the basis of issues like defence, education and health like the rest of us. Their vote is an unselfish one.[13]

In the United States the old people's lobby is a very strong voice politically, and older voters are more assertive on their own behalf. Another phenomenon observed there is the intensity of prejudice by the younger, affluent and active older people against those who are frail and dependent. There is no clear evidence of strong prejudice among young-old people against their elders in Britain. It could, however, be assumed that those who argue that the third age is a time of fun, opportunity and new learning believe that all this stops when you become more frail. Hiving off frail people to a fourth age is a rejection. The negative attitudes of one deprived group towards another yet more deprived group is demonstrated by the lack of attention that many disability organisations pay towards older people with disabilities, in spite of the fact that 70 per cent of disabled people are over retirement age. Another example is the way the women's movement has ignored older women. Barbara Macdonald is a longstanding activist now in her 70s. In her challenging book *Look Me in the Eye*,[14] she finds herself rejected by her feminist campaigner friends, with all kinds of excuses about her assumed deteriorating abilities. Sisterhood seemed to stop when she became old.

■ The professionals

Key professionals often share these negative attitudes. GPs can make a real improvement to the lives of elderly people. Many do. Yet poor service prevails more often than not. Any group, if they feel comfortable enough with you to voice their complaints, will tell sad stories about the way they have been treated. The chapter on health care looks at actual discriminatory practice, but older people can be very sensitive to the attitudes exemplified by the 'it's-only-your-age' approach. They know when they are being brushed off and not taken seriously. They know when doctors are not really interested. A German gerontologist,[15] in an article about old people written for GPs, wittily attacks stereotypes with facts, cartoons and photographs. She says: 'A pre-requisite of successful intervention and rehabilitation is correction of the negative attitude towards old age – including the image which doctors have of it. The doctor's expectations as to how the elderly patient should behave influence the actual behaviour of the elderly patient by non-verbal communication.' She also makes the interesting observation that the age of the doctor and the nurse partly determines their attitude. 'The older the doctor and the nurse, the more effectively they foster the self-reliant, independent behaviour in the elderly patient. Younger doctors and nurses, on the other hand, tend to encourage dependent behaviour and passivity on the part of older patients.'

An article in *Nursing Times*[16] points out that 'it is very easy for nurses caring for older people, especially in hospitals, to develop a rather jaundiced view of ageing. Exposed to elderly people who are in a state of acute or chronic physical illness, mental incapacity and increasing dependence, it is not surprising that nurses believe all elderly people experience the same decline.' The author is a health visitor and she describes her work in the community as having given her a 'positive and hopeful picture'. She enjoys working with older people who, in spite of disability, can organise their care workers to assist them in leading the lives they wish to lead. I think it is an unusual experience. The pressures of child-abuse work prevent most health visitors from doing more than minimal surveillance of the frailest old people. As a result, their attitudes towards old patients are undoubtedly influenced in the same way as their hospital-based colleagues.

Social workers are similarly influenced and exhibit the same pessimistic assumptions about the abilities of older people. Occupational therapists seem to be rare in their concentration on what people can do rather than what they are unable to do. The assessment tools of most professionals concentrate on the degree of impairment rather than the degree of potential. This is especially so when a diagnosis of dementia blinds workers to remaining skills.

These negative attitudes permeate decisions about crucial issues such as the allocation of resources, particularly the resources of skilled and experienced staff. Social-work training courses are characterised by negligible input on work with elderly people, and very few students choose this field for projects or placements. Most social services (in Scotland, social work) departments now have specialist teams for work with elderly people, but they include few qualified social workers. Although residential and day-care staff have been a priority target for training in many departments, the vast majority are untrained, except for the officers in charge. Who then is going to organise the packages of support required by the new structure of Community Care? It is unlikely to be qualified social workers. The consequence of all this is bound to be the persisting low status of this work. Trained and experienced social workers will continue to give priority to children at risk. Whatever one's views are about the most appropriate professional staff to work with older people, the reality is that social workers are the influential voice. Their priorities will be their departments' priorities.

It is a sad fact that most professionals do what interests them, rather than what most needs doing. The clearest evidence for this is the dearth of people keen to work with frail older people. Yet on any measure they are the most needy. They are numerically the largest group of people at risk, they present the most complex problems and their needs have the most impact on families and communities. One of the factors influencing the career decisions of professionals is opportunity for career advancement, which has been limited in this field until recently. It is just possible that the tide is now turning for social workers with the opportunity for specialisation and new roles in the Community Care service. There is a long way to go. The pages of unfilled job advertisements for psychogeriatricians in the *British Medical Journal* testifies to this, as does the increasing practice of splitting these posts into two areas of responsibility – part-time psychogeriatrics and part-time work with younger people – in order to made them more attractive.

The fact that professionals share the prevailing social attitudes is underlined by Alison Norman: 'The poor image of old age inevitably rubs off on those who are working in this field. Work with old people is not a prestigious occupation and there is a vicious circle in that jobs with low prestige tend to attract unambitious or less-skilled workers, or those who because of racial or social discrimination or competing domestic responsibilities cannot get work elsewhere.' She adds, however, 'there are of course many magnificent exceptions.'[17]

The field of housing is seldom scrutinised for its attitudes to older people. Yet the dramatic expansion of sheltered housing has probably contributed to the view of this age group being especially dependent. The very words 'sheltered housing' conjure up an image of elderly people who need protection. Politicians, local and national, have been able to claim great progress on the housing front, referring to the increasing numbers of sheltered housing units, yet conveniently ignoring that only about 5 per cent live in this kind of accommodation. Most older people do not need what is interestingly referred to as 'warden-controlled accommodation', although they seldom object to this extra facility. The impression has been given that they cannot live independently in ordinary housing. This may be changing. Staying Put and Care and Repair schemes, which are now the buzz concept in housing older people, demonstrate much more positive attitudes. They enable older people to remain in their own homes in comfort and security, assured that the buildings are warm and watertight. Except in the private sector, rented sheltered housing is being developed increasingly for people with special difficulties, such as extreme frailty or dementia: people who really do need a refuge.

An emerging key group of providers in this field are from the private sector. Since 1983, changes in social security regulations have given private-sector providers of residential and nursing-home care the confidence to expand because a subsidy was available for those residents without means or who ran out of money to pay the fees. The attitude of this sector, that the care of older people is an investment, is offensive to many people. The discussions between businessmen about profitability and how to maximise it, about dementia not being sufficiently profitable, about the sale of 'filled beds' – all these aspects are hard to take. It would be hypocritical to assert that the public sector provides better standards. Some private places are awful, but some longstay psychogeriatric wards are truly shameful. Few providers of longstay care for dependent people have provided really high-quality care, and we have to ask ourselves how far our attitudes to dependence in old age are affected by the kind of care that is offered. A study published by Age Concern Scotland asserts, that, 'to be dependent is to face the danger of being less than fully human because to be dependent is to live with the prospect of having our bodies cared for but our personal and social lives neglected or even dismissed as irrelevant.'[18] If longstay care for very dependent people was thoughtful and sensitive, would we all be so frightened of becoming very old? Would our attitudes to our future selves – which is what ageism is truly about – be so negative?

Finally, there must be a question about the lack of interest in older people on the part of the creative and recreational professions. Community education and sports organisations have, in the past, given attention to the over-50s, which implies that they are not interested at all in the very old. Arts groups have only just begun to take on board the fact that they have to be much more proactive if they are to tap the creativity of people who may be confined to their homes or only get out to day centres with help. The disabled lobby in the arts must take credit for the work they have done in making galleries more accessible, but there is a great deal more to do in order to encourage and demonstrate the creative talents of older people that undoubtedly exist.

▬ Action

The fact that this book is being published in Age Concern England's jubilee year is a major contribution to the British awareness of the problem of negative attitudes and age discrimination. It will generate a debate far beyond the world of those who work with older people.

There is a serious job to be done in raising the sensitivity of people to their own ageism. It needs to be something that is talked about in the same way that racism and sexism are talked about. While there is still a great deal to be done in both these fields, there are few people who are unaware of the terms and what they mean. Thoughtful people reflect on their own racism and sexism with real anxiety because these are matters that affect the way we relate to others. Exactly the same is true of ageism and everyone needs to be alert to their often unconscious ageist attitudes. I was dismayed by my own instant reaction when seeing a copy of a letter from the Director of Age Concern England to the Department of Health, asking for the age limits for blood donation to be extended above the present age limit of 65. I caught myself wondering how I would feel if I knew I was being transfused with the blood of someone of 85: would it be strong enough? On reflection, I was ashamed to have to remind myself that the age of the donor is an irrelevance; it is the quality of the blood that counts. This same knee-jerk reaction lies behind people's resistance to making retirement flexible. It is not age in itself which is important; it is people's ability to do the job. What is not acknowledged is the fact that it is very difficult to tell someone their blood is no good or they cannot do the job. It is so much easier to conform to arbitrary rules imposed by someone else on the basis of age. Is this to do with our inability as a nation to be direct when there is something unpalatable to say? Why is it that the Americans seem better able to cope with the idea of a flexible retirement age? We will not understand collective attitudes until we are more aware of individual ones.

Sexism became an issue partly because women were meeting in groups to examine their own experiences and attitudes. By doing so, they obtained a shared strength with which to challenge the attitudes of others. Of course, the challenge is when people who *are* sensitised to their own attitudes go back into a work or social setting where people are *not*. Changes percolate through gradually, much helped of course if there are major social and economic changes, such as the shortage of young people entering the labour market, which will inevitably open doors for women. It could open doors for older people too, but the foundations for changing attitudes have not been adequately laid.

Awareness of personal attitudes to ageing has to start young. We need to mix schoolchildren and older people more. Many children live a long way from their grandparents, so relationships with non-related older people need to be encouraged. Some schools already welcome older people into their classrooms. In my view, the better approach is when older people collaborate as fellow students or teachers, rather than the more common approach where schoolchildren organise tea parties or collect money or presents for 'needy old people'. It depends how it is done. Tea parties can be mutually enjoyable; they don't have to be events where 'active' children simply wait on 'passive' older people. Presents can be delivered as part of ongoing and mutually enjoyed relationships, but it is always preferable if the older people can return presents or hospitality. Unfortunately, they are sometimes too short of money for this to be possible.

Throughout adulthood we are constantly reinforcing our own ageist attitudes by blaming our own inadequacies on ageing. We cannot climb stairs quickly – 'it must be age'. This thoughtless response is so much easier than confronting the real reasons, as it has an inevitability about it. I have discovered that it offends people if you challenge this sort of remark. What their words really imply is that they do not want to think about why they are out of breath on stairs. However, attitudes are never changed without causing offence; hence the anger which often lies behind certain remarks about 'aggressive' women.

It is imperative that young and middle-aged adults confront their own and each other's ageism. This means, for example, being alert to ageist birthday cards; every birthday card for the over-40s implies waning competence, especially sexual competence. Something really needs to be done. Would a line in positive birthday cards sell? This constant reinforcement of the awfulness of ageing is not universal. In the Netherlands, for example, birthdays are celebrated at whatever age, with especially big celebrations at 50. Why can we British not have the same celebratory attitude? We seem increasingly able to talk about sex, but wholly unable to talk about our own ageing and our feelings about it.

How are we to raise awareness? The impetus will have to come from older people themselves. Sexism and racism did not become public issues because large numbers of men and of white people became aware of their negative attitudes to women and to black people. It is women and black people who force others to become aware of their own negative attitudes and the consequences these have. This challenge can be very threatening to men and to white people, partly because changing your interpretation of the world is an uncomfortable experience, and partly because a change of attitudes inevitably causes social change, and this in turn brings about a shift in power relationships. If there was recognition that older people have the capacity but are not given the opportunity for participation and decision-making in, for example, the way residential care and nursing homes are run, then a lot of things would have to change. More money, better staffing, better buildings and less control by the people in charge would result. It is much cheaper and easier to treat residents as passive and incapable. In West Germany, every residential facility has to have a residents' committee by law – this may not work in every case, but it speaks of a different attitude to the residents themselves.

The pensioner movement is only growing very slowly in Britain and it is hard to imagine the prosperous 20 per cent of pensioners feeling they had much in common with the 40 per cent who are completely dependent on state benefits. Yet there are encouraging signs. There are organisations for the United Kingdom, the Pensioners' Convention and the Pensioners' Liaison Forum, which bring together other national groups such as Pensioners' Voice, the British Pensioner and Trades Union Association and other retired members groups. Organised groups of older people meet in certain towns or regions of which the Strathclyde Elderly Forum is an excellent example. The older people involved in the dozens of local groups and the Strathclyde-wide executive committee have gained confidence, new skills and authority through their participation. This is especially noticeable in women who have often had no previous experience of public meetings or lobbying. The Strathclyde Elderly Forum has provided a voice for pensioners in the way local services are, or are not, provided. Many local groups have also set about organising their own services. Govan Action for Pensioners, for example, runs an advice centre in a local flat, so coffee and comfortable chairs are available too. A huge and successful organisation like this does not happen without resources, especially with older people on low incomes and in variable health. Back-up has been provided by social work and community education staff and the Forum now has an urban-aid grant to provide staffing to assist its work in especially deprived areas. This organisation challenges every stereotype: members are articulate, effective and unembarrassed about using personal experiences to justify their claims.

One lesson we can learn from the Strathclyde Elderly Forum is the importance of the attitudes of community workers. It was a combination of the determination of groups of older people and the active support from local workers that enabled the organisation to develop. This underlines the importance of training schemes in which professionals have opportunities to meet older people who are in charge of their lives, who have something to say and who are not being seen simply because they have overwhelming problems. Social work training that includes talks from older people, however old and frail, about the experience of being old can change attitudes fundamentally. A woman of 99 who lived in an old people's home was a regular lecturer to one social work course. A group of medical students, who spent two weeks recording older people's assessments of this century, discovered that they were fascinating and not at all preoccupied with illness. Nurses, who watch groups of older people getting together to role-play interactions with professionals, learn a great deal about the barriers which busy professionals put up in order to avoid real communication.

There are many ways to learn about old age from older people, ways which put them into the 'expert' role. A recently widowed friend of mine, well into her 80s, writes to say that she 'was asked to speak on bereavement-coping at a conference of social workers and has had two more bookings as a result.' Barbara Macdonald, herself in her 70s, gives an excellent list of suggestions to assist younger women in relating to her and her peer group in a non-ageist way.[19]

The vogue for advocacy and self-advocacy has been slow to develop for older people. They are very familiar concepts in the field of people with learning difficulties. Advocacy projects are beginning to emerge, with young-old people often acting as advocates for people with illnesses like dementia or stroke who cannot articulate their needs. Self-advocacy requires training and support for inarticulate people to learn how to voice their needs and wishes. I once attended a talk at which a group of people with learning difficulties described how they hated being called 'mentally handicapped'. It made a lasting impression on me. There may be all kinds of professional practices which frail and inarticulate older people hate, but which, without support, they would be unable to articulate.

One of the fundamental ways of changing attitudes is through information. Often, negative attitudes are based on misinformation. A commonly held view is that 'we're all of us . . . moving . . . into the category of those who don't know what day it is.' Most people think dementia (or senility as it is wrongly called) is inevitable. In fact, only one in ten of us will suffer from it. Yet a taxi driver told me recently that more money should be spent on Aids than on dementia because more people would die from it. 91,000 people have dementia in Scotland and although many will die of other causes, vastly more will die of dementia than the few hundred dying of Aids. It is not helpful to pit one tragic illness against another in the battle for resources, but the level of public ignorance in this case is significant.

Research which clarifies the way older people learn, or the extent to which they are mentally rigid, provides invaluable ammunition for more positive attitudes. Research comparing young and older people's attitudes to sexual morality has found that both groups displayed the same degree of flexibility. The accompanying report summarises other related research: 'These images of older persons as clinging to the past and as being resistant to change reflect two widely-held assumptions about ageing. The first is that social and political attitudes tend to become more conservative as persons grow older . . . the second position suggests that attitude change ceases to occur. . . . Some recent evidence, however, is beginning to cast considerable doubt on the empirical validity of these views. Findings from these few studies provide tentative support for the conclusion that there is no inevitable drift towards conservative social and political attitudes with ageing, nor is ageing necessarily associated with attitudinal rigidity or inflexibility.'[20]

Age Concern Scotland has produced two invaluable quizzes which address some of the myths that surround ageing and give the research evidence to combat (and occasionally support) them.[21] Researchers have reviewed the evidence in order to establish the extent to which the usually gloomy predictions of a huge dependent population are justified. On the whole they feel such predictions are not justified and, indeed, the evidence is of a much greater degree of fitness and independence than is generally acknowledged.[22] This presents a dilemma for organisations campaigning on behalf of older people. It cannot be denied that we need more resources to improve the quality of life of very frail older people. They become invisible and ignored too quickly if their needs are not constantly presented to the public and to politicians. However, in emphasising their dependence it is only too easy to diminish what they can and do contribute. Fundraising by major charities for older people must emphasise both sides of the picture if they are not to reinforce harmful stereotypes. Fundraising letters go to upper-income groups, many of whom are important and influential people; their voice is vital. The King's Fund Centre has produced an excellent and much-needed paper on publicising the needs of people with disabilities.[23]

In the effort to distribute accurate information, keeping journalists and politicians well informed is absolutely crucial. Both Age Concern England and Age Concern Scotland have produced wallet-sized fact cards which have been widely distributed and used.

Individual attitude change can be reinforced by an organisation's commitment to positive attitudes. It is extraordinary how few professional organisations have a code of ethics like social workers: 'Basic to the profession of social work is the recognition of the value and dignity of every human being, irrespective of origin, race, status, sex, sexual orientation, age, belief or contribution to society. The profession accepts a responsibility to encourage and facilitate the self-realisation of each individual person with due regard for the interest of others.' Very few social services/work departments have a statement of principle for their work with older people. Very few health and Community Care plans – joint or otherwise – begin with principles against which the plan can be judged. These are important opportunities to tell staff what is expected of them, as well as old people what they can expect.

In conclusion, despite all that has been said, it must be emphasised that attitudes are as much affected by reality as affecting reality. Not until society's approach to older people has changed – the approach of government departments, professional groups and the media, for example – will our own attitudes to ageing change. That is why the rest of this book is so important. We have to challenge and defeat ageist attitudes in Britain today so that older people can feel proud to be old.

NO SENSE OF URGENCY
AGE DISCRIMINATION IN HEALTH CARE

MELANIE HENWOOD

Melanie Henwood joined the King's Fund Institute as a Fellow in Health Policy Analysis in July 1989 after working at the Family Policy Studies Centre since 1983. Her previous publications have addressed family care and community care in relation to older people and she is currently researching alternative forms of long term care for this group.

As we move towards the close of the twentieth century, survival into old age and extreme old age is no longer unusual. With up to one third of a lifetime now being spent in retirement, increasing attention is being paid to the quality of that life. A key element of this must be good health. Yet, we find, not only is there widespread discrimination against older people in the provision of health care, but they are also the victims of restricted assumptions about the quality of health which can be expected in old age. The particular health needs of later life are perceived as a low priority, with older people actually being excluded from services which are taken for granted by younger patients.

Attitudes to old age

The negative image of old age as a time of increasing dependency is discussed throughout this book and is evident in many assumptions about the nature of health in later life. Typically, old age is viewed as a period of 'inevitable deterioration' and 'irreversible decline', with older people becoming increasingly frail and sick. But old age itself is *not* a disease, and many of the conditions associated with it are neither inevitable nor universal. While depression, incontinence, dementia, general aches and pains, and particular illnesses are more *likely* to develop they are not caused by old age itself.

All living organisms age, undergoing certain physiological changes as they do so. This primary process of ageing, known as senescence, is simply the biological changes which begin as growth and development end. However, while all people experience similar changes, the degree of change is very wide-ranging and there is considerable variation both between individuals and between socio-cultural groups. Changes take place in appearance and perception – sight, hearing and taste all deteriorate from middle age. Muscular-skeletal changes also occur, with an average loss of 50 per cent of muscle tissue by the age of 80. The loss of bone mass is recognised as a universal characteristic of ageing – beginning at around 30 years in women and 50 in men – although there are wide differences in the amount and rate of loss. The risk of fractures increases with the thinning of bones, and the incidence of certain fractures – notably hip and vertebral – rises dramatically with old age and the onset for some of osteoporosis. While these general observations about the ageing process can be made, there are extensive gaps in our knowledge about ageing. In particular, the lack of longitudinal studies of older people in Britain is a major deficiency.[1]

In the same way that notions of old age are structured by social and economic policies, concepts of health are similarly socially constructed; there is no simple definition of either health or illness. Rather, there are a range of perspectives, but the one which has tended to dominate health services is the 'disease model' which is 'concerned with health as the absence of illness or disease, rather than the promotion of positive health.' The interaction of this model of health with stereotypes of old age, which are generally negative and treat older people as a homogeneous group, can have profound consequences. Some argue that it 'produces a tendency to classify all old people as suffering from incurable diseases.'[2] But the normal biological processes of ageing are not synonymous with either disease or loss of function.

▬ Health needs in old age

While it needs to be emphasised that old age does not automatically mean ill health and dependency, nonetheless there are clear associations between advancing years and increasing ill health and disability. Recent information is provided by the General Household Survey, and the Office of Population Censuses and Surveys (OPCS) disability surveys. In 1986, 61 per cent of men aged over 65, and 65 per cent of women, reported a 'long-standing illness'. Acute illness episodes were also significant, restricting the activities of men over 75 for an average 47 days each year, and of women for an average 61 days each year – compared with 23 days and 29 days respectively for men and women of all ages. Older people also consult their GP about twice as often as younger people.[3]

The OPCS report on disability, published in 1988, estimated there were six million people in Britain with some level of disability. 70 per cent of these were aged at least 60, and among the most severely disabled the very elderly predominated.[4] The reality of such disability is evident in the limitations it imposes on aspects of everyday life. In 1986 almost half the people aged over 85, for example, were unable to go out of doors and walk down the road on their own, and almost a third were unable to manage stairs.

It is important to emphasise that older people should not be regarded *en masse* as ill, frail or in terminal decline. Nonetheless, the high incidence of illness and disability, especially among the most elderly, underlines the need for positive health care and treatment. Many conditions associated with old age can be treated and alleviated, if not cured. There is, however, a widespread opinion that this is not the case, and that illness in old age is 'just one of those things to be put up with.' The OPCS rightly pointed out that their disability survey covered a wide spectrum of incapacity and that 'sweeping conclusions' about dependency should be avoided. However, this was a different point to that made by Minister for the Disabled, Nicholas Scott, who commented that it was unwise to view all older people in the survey as disabled because '. . . many consider the relatively minor limitations of hearing, vision or movement recorded by the survey as in fact normal for their age.' These 'relatively minor' limitations can restrict older people's participation in everyday life and social interaction. They can make it impossible to read a newspaper, walk down the road, go shopping, listen to the radio or join in conversation. To view this situation as 'normal' is unacceptable, especially when other people of the same age do not suffer in this way, and when there is considerable evidence that much can be done to overcome or alleviate the handicap.

The concerns of older people

Despite the objective evidence concerning levels of ill health and disability in old age, more than 60 per cent of people aged over 65 describe their health as 'good' or 'very good'. It is likely that these perceptions of health reflect expectations that a high degree of ill health and discomfort should be accepted in old age. This apparent equanimity, however, is belied by evidence that health and health care are major concerns of older people. A recent poll conducted by Gallup of attitudes among people over the age of 65 found considerable anxiety about health care in old age. When considering the implications of longer life expectations, and selecting from a pre-coded list, concerns over health were second only to those about income. Almost 75 per cent of those polled feared poverty, while 55 per cent believed that the National Health Service would fail to put sufficient resources into keeping older people fit and healthy. Such concern was expressed alongside an expectation of deteriorating health. Almost one in three people felt that 'failing health' best summarised their thoughts about old age.[5]

In the light of these concerns, and the dismal outlook of many, it is perhaps unsurprising that only 28 per cent agreed that helping older people to live as long as possible should be a priority issue. Immortality holds little appeal if it is accompanied by increased ill health, inadequate attention to those needs by the health service, and a society with a diminishing regard for older people – which almost half the surveyed group believed.

▬ Demographic demands

Misconceptions about ill health in old age – and the perception of older people themselves that poor health is inevitable – form the backdrop to growing political concern over the health care needs of an ageing population.

Between 1901 and 1981 the number of people in Britain aged over 65 rose from 1.7 million to almost 8 million, increasing as a proportion of the total population from less than 5 per cent to 15 per cent. The dramatic increase in the population aged over 65 has now slowed, but the growth in the number of very elderly people (aged over 75 and over 85) is now particularly significant. The likely doubling of numbers of people aged over 85 between 1981 and 2001 is striking; by the same year almost half the elderly population will be at least 75.

There are conflicting perspectives on whether greater longevity will of itself give rise to increased disability, but without significant improvements in health, average levels of dependency and chronic illness will in future rise simply because growing proportions of the population will be extremely old. For example, while in 1985 15 per cent of those aged over 75 were unable to bath without help, on the basis of current trends this will be true of 17 per cent by 2001, an increase of almost 188,000 people, simply because of the increased proportion of those actually aged over 85.

Much of the political reaction to these trends has been unhelpful and alarmist. The 'demographic and pension time bombs' are much over-used phrases, and the Health Advisory Service's emotive discussion of 'the rising tide' of the frail elderly population reflects similar demographic despair.[6] This negative and problem-focused view of the ageing population is nothing new. The 1942 Beveridge report on social insurance gave special consideration to 'the problem of age' and the 'intolerable financial burden' which growing numbers of older people were seen to present. Not only were their needs felt to threaten the living standards of other groups, but it was argued that these needs should be given less priority: 'It is dangerous to be in any way lavish to old age, until adequate provision has been assured for all other vital needs, such as the prevention of disease and the adequate nutrition of the young.'[7]

■ The provision of health care in old age

In the light of such increasing need or demand, the implications for health care are far reaching. If discrimination is not to increase, questions about the volume and quality of health services for older people will become increasingly urgent and must be faced. Certainly such pressures and demands point to the need to make both prevention and treatment of chronic diseases a priority.

The concerns of older people about their future health care probably reflect beliefs about modern medicine and priorities within the medical profession. Only 13 per cent of the Gallup respondents thought that pioneering new forms of surgery should be a priority for the National Health Service. They were much more concerned about efforts to prevent illness, and to improve the quality of life of people incurably ill.

This raises issues about the direction of the National Health Service and the continued dominance of acute services in the face of the increasing needs of growing numbers of people with chronic and degenerative conditions, which an editorial in *The Economist* recently described as 'types of misery that make old age worse than it need be.'[8]

One of the central strengths of the enduring popular appeal of the National Health Service has been the belief in its provision of comprehensive services on the basis of need, rather than the ability to pay or other restrictive criteria. The principle that all individuals are of equal moral worth should mean equality of access to services, and equal quality of treatment for all individuals. Few people perhaps would disagree with this as a moral principle or ethic but, in practice, the reality has not matched the ideal. Resources are finite, and choices have to be made between competing priorities and needs. Implicitly, many decisions may have been made that disadvantage older people. The ethical and the economic perspective present sharply differentiated positions.[9]

Two major theoretical issues underlie the reality of health care provision for older people. The first concerns the limits to intervention for individual patients; the second concerns the relative claims of older people and other citizens. These two areas are not entirely distinct, but it may be useful to examine them separately.

A contributor to a recent American volume on the ageing population described health care in an ageing society as 'a moral dilemma'. He argued that 'experience is teaching us that medicine can keep some elderly people alive for longer than is of any benefit to them.' There is, he suggested, 'the increasing necessity to make painful moral choices in the care of the dying elderly as a class, particularly among that growing number who end their days incompetent, incontinent, and grossly incapacitated, more dead than alive.'[10] The maxim that life should not be extended at the cost of worsening it has an obvious appeal: it is also a gross over-simplification. The optimal moment for ceasing medical intervention is rarely this clear-cut, but obviously there are tensions between attempts to prolong life, and the quality of life in the extra days attained. Issues about 'dignity in death' are complex and rarely fully aired. Many states in the United States recognise the authority of a 'living will', which gives prior authorisation for the cessation of life-prolonging medical intervention in the event of terminal illness or irreversible brain damage. In Britain, such a declaration has no legal status, and decisions about continuing heroic treatments, even where there is no prospect of recovery or benefit, are left very much to clinical judgement.[11]

The second major issue concerns both implicit and explicit discrimination against elderly people, both as individuals and as a group. While life expectancy has extended, it appears to have been at the price of a longer period and a greater proportion of life being spent in chronic sickness. At the same time, within the National Health Service, it has been acute and curative services which have been developed, despite attempts to shift the balance towards preventive and caring services directed at chronic conditions. Older people are not the only group to be disadvantaged by such trends. The phrase 'Cinderella services' was coined to describe the relative paucity of care for the mentally ill, people with learning difficulties and people with physical disabilities as well as elderly people. These groups share the characteristics of having long-term and chronic needs. Because of the scale of increase in the older population, however, it is the very old and frail who are seen to represent the greatest challenge to the health and community care services.

Services for people with disabilities have been a low priority over many years, and the inadequacy of provision – both in quantity and quality – is well known. Older people are particularly disadvantaged by this situation because of their greater likelihood of disability. It has been suggested that 'aids and equipment supply is the single most confused area of service provision for disabled people.' Health authorities have responsibility for nursing aids, and social service departments are responsible for aids to daily living. In practice, these distinctions are rarely so clear, and many severely disabled people will have needs for multiple support which cross these agency boundaries. The result is 'a complex, time-consuming and often frustrating business for people with disabilities.' Long delays in the supply of equipment are commonplace, and poor assessment frequently leads to inappropriate or inadequate aids being supplied.[12]

Moreover, failure to provide adequate services means that less is being achieved for many elderly people than is possible. Improved rehabilitation techniques, for example, mean that many elderly stroke patients can now achieve greater functional improvement than was previously thought possible. However, shortage of physiotherapy and other services, together with rapid hospital discharge, militates against such results being achieved.

The 1979 Royal Commission on the National Health Service estimated that an annual growth of 1 per cent in public expenditure was required simply to keep pace with demographic pressures. Recent public expenditure White Papers have allowed an annual 2 per cent for such changes as well as to take account of the increased costs of technological progress, but the adequacy of this allowance is in doubt. The Social Services Committee of the House of Commons continues to stress that 'the Government should acknowledge that improving health services and expanding services as dictated by the twin demands of demography and technology will not be cheap.'[13]

The domination of acute services and the parallel increases in high-tech medicine have considerable influence on people's expectations of what is appropriate and possible in health care. Dramatic life-saving techniques, organ transplants and similar developments have popular appeal. They are also more likely to be directed at people below retirement age; indeed, the latest challenge in micro-surgery appears to be successful operations on ever younger patients. At the beginning of 1990, for example, there was a much publicised case of heart surgery carried out on an infant still in the womb. The baby subsequently died in intensive care.

The need to ration health care resources is a fact of life for the National Health Service, as for any modern health care system. Questions about *how* care is rationed, however, are crucial. If services were to be provided on purely egalitarian terms, all people who might benefit from any given treatment would be able to do so. However, given finite resources, concepts of effectiveness and efficiency must be considered alongside concepts of need. In other words, the principle is that 'within a fixed budget, health care resources should be allocated so as to achieve the greatest aggregate of well-being for patients.'[14] However, how such a judgement can be made is controversial. The view expressed by health economists such as Alan Maynard is still one which is rarely articulated quite so starkly: 'We have to demonstrate much more clearly that the spending involved in care for elderly people is spending which is efficient. Until we demonstrate that, the case for increasing expenditure on elderly people has to be very modest, and related to what evidence we have about whether it will improve their welfare.'[15]

One concept which has been the focus of much debate in evaluating efficiency is that of the 'Quality Adjusted Life Year' or QALY developed by the health economist, Alan Williams. An attempt is made to value the resources required for a given treatment against the years of better quality of life it will produce. Whatever the limitations intrinsic to the QALY approach, the approach itself is inherently discriminatory. A report of a working party on the ethical dimension of choice in health care observed that 'any procedure that includes counting extra years of life as part of the benefit of medical procedures will risk shifting resources away from the elderly and towards younger age groups.'[16]

The QALY approach is formally egalitarian, but its application introduces bias against older people. There will generally be fewer life years added by the treatment of older people and, similarly, those with a low quality of life – predominantly older people – will be disadvantaged by a QALY approach to life-saving measures.

The respective rights of young and old – whether for health or welfare and income support – have not generally been articulated as sharply in this country as they have in the United States. The prevalence of 'burden of dependency' attitudes to old age are, however, reflections of a similar perspective. One American commentator has expressed the following view: 'the skewing effect of an ageing society is that the economic imbalances caused by the provision of health care for the elderly potentially threaten the welfare of younger generations and of society as a whole ... the stage is set for a profound confrontation.'[17]

Such 'a profound confrontation' has not yet occurred in Britain, perhaps in part because issues of cost and economics have been more easily concealed within a universal health care service such as the National Health Service, than they are within more market-driven systems. Questions of cost, however, are likely to become more explicit in the 'internal market' being developed within the National Health Service in the 1990s.

▬ Discrimination in screening

If rationing or discriminatory decisions in health care are rarely made explicit within the National Health Service, such judgements are nonetheless made, and have typically been left to individual doctors. In some areas, however, guidelines *are* more explicit. The field of screening is one example. Despite the obvious appeal of the 'prevention is better than cure' maxim, the matter of screening apparently healthy populations for hidden or unreported disease is controversial. Much screening is experimental in nature, and of dubious – or unproven – benefit. There has, however, been considerable work in developing the concept of 'opportunistic' case-finding, which for older people means identifying those likely to need help or to develop health care problems. Such case-finding, it is suggested by some, should be applied annually to all people aged over 65. The belief underlying such proposals is that many older people are only referred for treatment at a late stage of dependency when treatment is less effective and more expensive. However, evidence suggests that such general screening may be inappropriate.

A review of screening and preventive care of older people by the Royal College of General Practitioners published in 1987 indicated particular 'high risk' groups for whom screening might be targeted. These risk indicators took account both of social and medical variables – for example, elderly patients receiving repeat prescriptions, or those recently widowed.[18]

A 1986 report from the British Medical Association also suggested that universal screening is 'probably not justified', and that it could 'alarm some elderly people unnecessarily.'[19] Nonetheless, it was also pointed out that screening *could* be effective in uncovering treatable conditions which sufferers were otherwise likely to put up with as simply the inevitable consequence of old age. An attempt at geriatric screening in general practice in 1979, for example, found 145 patients aged over 70 with 400 conditions between them. More than a third of these conditions had been previously undetected, and two-thirds of the illnesses were manageable, while half of them were totally cleared up by treatment.[20]

The new contract for General Practitioners now stipulates that all patients aged over 75 should be offered an annual check up and home visit where, if possible, assistance can be offered to cope with any undetected functional handicaps. The functional rather than case-finding approach to this screening raises different issues. It does offer some opportunity to counteract the disadvantage many older people experience in access to health services, and in the reluctance of doctors to make home visits.

There are strong arguments, however, for case-finding screening for particular conditions. Osteoporosis is one example. The Office of Health Economics observes that 'osteoporotic fractures in the elderly present a major health care and social problem which is largely preventable. The consequences of these fractures are enormous both socio-economically and as regards morbidity and mortality.'[21] More than 46,000 people in England and Wales suffer hip fractures each year – 60 per cent of them are women aged at least 75. About a quarter of these people die as a result of their injuries and complications, and many more fail to regain full mobility. As well as the extreme distress and loss of life this condition can cause, the hospital costs of dealing with the fractures are some £160 million a year, and a fifth of orthopaedic beds are occupied by such cases.[22]

The risk factors for osteoporosis are well known, yet despite its prevalence – perhaps 25 per cent of women are at risk of osteoporotic fractures – and the severe consequences of such fractures, little priority is currently attached to developing preventive and screening approaches to this condition. Such apathy is indicative of the generally low emphasis and under-investment in health education and preventive medicine in Britain.[23] Without such a preventive drive, the cost will rise dramatically with the growth of the very elderly population. The Royal College of Physicians, for example, calculate that if present trends continue, the incidence of hip fracture will increase to an annual 94,000 by 2006.[24] This state of affairs is an example of discrimination against the needs of older people; it not only causes great suffering but unnecessary economic costs.

The logic of any screening method is two-fold. First, that it detects the affected or at-risk groups, and second that these can then be referred for suitable treatment. In the case of osteoporosis there *are* preventive therapies, but insufficient research has been undertaken into the costs and benefits of Hormone Replacement Therapy (HRT), calcitonin therapy, and mineral supplements. The Office of Health Economics suggest that the benefits to be gained from HRT 'are far in excess of any known risks associated with its use.' The hospital cost alone of hip fractures in England and Wales was £128 million in 1985. In 1988 the total cost to the National Health Service of all osteoporotic fractures was an estimated £500 million. It is likely that HRT for post-menopausal women would reduce hip fractures by 50 per cent.

The example of osteoporosis helps to illustrate that it is not simply older *people* who suffer from inadequate and discriminating health care, more specifically it is older *women.* Because women generally outlive men, most very elderly people are women (almost 70 per cent of those aged over 75 and 75 per cent of those over 85), and it is conditions affecting older women where questions about equity in health care are particularly obvious.

If osteoporosis is one area where people suffer particularly because of inadequate attention to screening methods, cervical cancer provides an example of where screening processes *do* exist, but specifically exclude older citizens. Some 40 per cent of deaths from cancer of the cervix in England occur in women aged 65 or over. Department of Health guidelines, however, exclude screening or regular follow-up of women over 65, and none of the 94 per cent of District Health Authorities with a recall system includes women of this age. A recent analysis of such practices in *The Lancet* concluded that 'there seems to be no reason to exclude older women from regular screening for cancer of the cervix. On the contrary, since a high proportion of this age group have never had a smear or no recent smear, screening of this age group would have substantial benefits.'[25] It cannot be assumed that women over 65 would have had an adequate screening history and therefore can be forgotten, or that there is no point in regular follow-up of older patients. In fact the screening rate of women in the excluded group has been low over the last 20 years – some 50-80 per cent of older women have never had a smear. The natural history of cervical cancer among older women is uncertain, but 'that little is known about the natural history of cancer of the cervix does not seem to have been an obstacle to the introduction of screening programmes for younger women.'[26]

Opportunistic screening would, it is believed, identify more cases at an earlier stage. Women aged over 65 would benefit most, with a 63 per cent improvement in five-year mortality. To deny older women access to routine screening is both contra-indicated and explicitly discriminatory.

Sometimes screening which is not available to older women may not have proven effectiveness for the group to whom it is offered. Screening for breast cancer is usually offered to women aged 50-64. It is generally assumed that it is not cost-effective to screen either younger or older women, but the achievements of *any* screening in this area are unclear. Maureen Roberts, the late Director of the Edinburgh Breast Screening Project, observed that screening 'is not offering any certainty of cure or normal life to the women who attend, merely a prolongation of years for a few. Not only that: we cannot predict who will have those extra years.'[27]

Breast screening is a politically sensitive issue. Considerable resources are expended on screening and evaluation programmes. Yet it seems likely that resources would actually be better used in other prevention programmes. Such programmes should be directed at lifestyle rather than disease detection, and targeted at improving the health of women of all ages.

Discrimination against elderly people, however, appears to be a general feature of cancer treatment. About half of all new malignancies occur in people aged over 70, yet such cancers are often poorly treated and little understood. A recent paper in *The Lancet* observed that people aged over 70 are excluded from almost all clinical trials of cancer treatment, with the result that elderly patients 'receive either untested treatments, inadequate treatments, or even none at all, at the whim of their clinician.'[28]

Many erroneous assumptions are made both about the nature of cancer in older people and the response to treatment. The under-treatment of cancer in older people means that many tumours which could be controlled or cured are not. The authors of the paper do not suggest ignoring the age of the patient, quite the reverse: 'criteria appropriate for younger patients may not be suitable in the elderly, for whom effective stabilisation of disease, a partial remission, or a complete remission of short duration may be sufficient to achieve worthwhile prolongation of life with an acceptable quality of life.' They argue that the same rigour should be applied to the study of older patients with cancer as for younger – 'only then will we see strikingly reduced population mortality and improved quality of life for older patients with cancer.'[29]

■ **Health care and elderly people in the future**
This chapter has considered some of the dimensions of the likely future needs for health care among older people, and has examined practices which discriminate against those needs by comparison with other age groups. What is likely to happen in the future, and – in particular – what are the likely consequences of the changes in the health service? Little specific attention was paid to older people in the White Paper, *Working for Patients,*[30] nor to the effect on them of changes in the GP contract, but the implications of the changes for the care of older patients may be significant.

Some general practices will choose to become budget holders, and the unattractiveness of older patients to these practices may be considerable.[31] The potential cost of older patients, and the demands they would make on cash-limited budgets, would be obvious disincentives. Similarly, non-budget-holding practices may be affected by increased requirements for home visits, and fears – despite Government assurance – that drug budgets will be restricted. If older people are rejected by or struck off the lists of GPs, access to local care could deteriorate. Already many experience difficulties in getting to their GP;[32] having to change to a more distant practice would disadvantage them further.

The promotion of the 'internal market' in health care has uncertain consequences for older people. Contracts may be developed with hospitals further afield, but few patients would choose to enter a hospital far from home. Not only will travel for treatment be onerous (including post-operative outpatient care), but visits from older friends and family would also be more difficult. The discharge process from distant hospitals also increases problems of liaison with rehabilitative and community services. The overall emphasis on cost and efficiency in the reformed National Health Service is likely to increase pressures for further reducing the length of hospital stays, and once again this may be to the detriment of older patients.

The place of geriatric medicine within the new arrangements for the National Health Service also remains unclear. Geriatric and psychogeriatric care remain low status and poorly resourced specialties. Much has been achieved in geriatric medicine, and a multi-disciplinary approach is well established in many places. Psychogeriatric care is of increasing importance with the rising incidence of senile dementia – yet some health authorities are still without even a single psychogeriatrician, let alone an adequate level of staffing for their elderly population.[33]

The care of elderly people will not inevitably deteriorate in the future, but the potential for this to be the case underlines the importance of close monitoring of the impact of *Working for Patients* on the future quality of the National Health Service.

New developments in Community Care also have major implications for the future care of older people. As *Caring for People* acknowledged, 'community care is about the health as well as the social needs of the population.'[34] The distinction between health and social care is not an easy one to make, but it is likely to become increasingly problematic.

The rapid expansion of private nursing-home care over the last decade is well known and has enabled very old people to move from large wards into more homely environments. In the future, admission to nursing or residential care will be conditional on assessment, and with local authorities becoming responsible for the costs of residents requiring public support, such admissions will come under critical financial scrutiny. It is likely that disputes over the respective responsibilities of health and local authorities will intensify, and without substantial investment by the National Health Service in continuing care many older people will remain in inappropriate hospital care.

Conclusions

It is a major triumph of the twentieth century that many more people survive to a ripe old age, but there can be no room for complacency. The quality of life in the later years is often abysmal. Moreover, substantial improvements could often be easily achieved. The poor mobility, fear of falling and resulting social isolation which is experienced by many older people, for example, could often be improved simply by better foot care and chiropody services. More attention to auditory and visual needs, and the provision of appropriate aids and adaptations can also make a great difference to quality of life and confidence. Other needs, however, demand a much more substantial response.

There is no doubt that the chronic and long-term needs of older people receive inadequate attention at present. Much of this reflects the entrenched acute-service bias of the National Health Service, and major change would have far-reaching implications. Greater attention must be paid to both alleviating existing chronic conditions among older people, and to preventive strategies throughout the life cycle.

Ethical debates about the quality of life and the limits to medical intervention are certain to become more pressing as frontiers are rolled back on what is technically possible. This has implications for people of all ages, but the tensions are especially clear in relation to old age. The issues are complex and multi-faceted, but a concentration on economic questions – as in the application of the QALY approach – must not be allowed to overshadow humanitarian considerations.

Questions about equal access to services and equal rights to treatment also raise important issues about the value of particular interventions. Rather than arguing that elderly people should automatically have a right to all forms of screening, or other selective treatments, we should ask whether such programmes should be in operation at all, and if the resources would not be better deployed in alternative approaches.

More needs to be known about the 'normal' process of ageing. Longitudinal data would be invaluable in providing this essential information in Britain. Too many practitioners are inclined to dismiss levels of illness and disability as a fact of life in old age, when often it need not be so.

There is likely to be a widening gap in modern medicine between what is technically possible, what is financially feasible , and what is ethically justifiable or desirable. Difficult decisions have to be made in the rationing of scarce resources. If older people are not to be disadvantaged, and not to be treated as a separate class defined solely on the basis of age, it is vital that the debate about rationing care is a public one; and that principles about equality and individual value are considered alongside economic imperatives.

4 THE BENEFITS OF OLD AGE?

AGE DISCRIMINATION AND SOCIAL SECURITY

ALAN WALKER

Alan Walker is Professor of Social Policy and Chairperson of the Department of Sociological Studies at Sheffield University and has published numerous books and articles on ageing and social policy. He is currently engaged in research studies on the social care of elderly people and the employment of older workers. He is also an active campaigner against poverty and for welfare rights, and was co-founder and is now Honorary Secretary of the Disability Alliance.

I write this chapter with a deep personal commitment to social justice for all older people. I regard age discrimination, or ageism, as being as offensive and pernicious as sexism and racism. Indeed, unlike those other forms of discrimination, ageism has yet to attract the attention of policy makers and the public, so deeply engrained is it in our thoughts and actions. My own research over nearly 20 years, as well as that of others, has confirmed the ageist nature of British society. This research shows that there is an urgent need for social policies to overcome widespread age discrimination if older people are to be allowed to play their full role in society and realise their full potential. This goal must, surely, be regarded as the very minimum necessary both for a civilised society and for us to begin to secure social justice for this group.

This chapter focuses on the ways in which age discrimination is both a product of and manifested in the social security system. Ageist assumptions underlie policies in the social security field and not surprisingly therefore, these policies reinforce age discrimination. The clear implication of this analysis is that ageism is created primarily by social and economic institutions and their policies, rather than by chronological age itself.[1] Of course, social security is only one aspect of the apparatus of government social policy and, equally, the Government is only one part, though an important one, of the overall social and economic processes whereby ageism has been embedded in twentieth-century Britain. However, the social security system has played a central role in these processes as an element of government economic management, particularly where it has been used to support employment policies aimed at the exclusion of increasing numbers of older people from the labour market. In recent years the increasingly rigid age division of British society has been underpinned by social security, including pensions, policy.

It may be argued that to focus on social security is to overlook other sources of income in old age. Although a fuller account would include a detailed analysis of all sources of income, the plain fact is that by far the largest source of pensioners' income is social security, comprising 60 per cent, with the retirement pension alone making up 49 per cent of pensioner income.[2] This reliance on the state demonstrates the impact of exclusion from the labour market – only 9 per cent of the total income of older people comes from employment. In addition, even though a fifth of total income is derived from occupational pensions, the vast majority of pensioners rely on social security either for all or for a significant proportion of their income: two-thirds of them receive 80 per cent or more of their income from this source. It is only among the richest pensioners, who receive some very high proportions of previous earnings from their occupational pensions, that this source of income dwarfs social security. Thus, in the top tenth of pensioner income groups, social security contributes only a quarter of gross income. This means that for a small, privileged minority there is no effective, or only slight, age discrimination in income levels. Unfortunately, as this chapter shows, for the majority the impact of ageism is all too clear.

The social creation of ageism

As I have argued at length elsewhere, retirement is both the leading form of age discrimination and the driving force behind the wider development of ageism in modern societies.[3] The long-term decline in the participation of older people, particularly older men, in the workforce cannot be attributed to changes in the individual characteristics of older people themselves – their health, attitudes to work and so on. Nor can this trend be understood simply on the basis of the preferences expressed by older workers. In Britain and other industrial societies, retirement policies have been used by employers, including the Government, to reduce and re-structure their workforces in response to both the constant pressure to increase productivity and cyclical changes in the demand for labour. Thus, retirement may be seen as an age discriminatory social process designed to exclude older people *en masse* from the workforce. Indeed much of the impetus behind the development of retirement was provided by the economic, medical and managerial theories of the late-nineteenth and early-twentieth centuries concerning the industrial efficiency of younger and older workers. The most famous of these was F W Taylor's theory of scientific management, set out in a series of publications in the early part of this century.[4] These theories were themselves ageist; they favoured the young, and portrayed older workers as inefficient burdens. Although the early scientific theories about declining productivity in older age groups are now discredited, these prejudices still exert a powerful influence.[5] Not surprisingly, trades unions have co-operated in the development of this age discriminatory policy, believing it to be in the interests of their older and younger members alike.

▬ Pensions before Beveridge

The growth of pensions and other social security provision for older people this century is inextricably linked to the promotion of retirement. Social security ensured that the costs of mass retirement were kept as low as possible and were spread over the whole population rather than falling only on employers. In doing this, the social security system has helped to encourage and justify age discrimination, providing a model for the private sector to emulate. Equally, of course, pensions were essential for older people who were dismissed summarily on grounds of age. Indeed the origins of the campaign for old age pensions lay in this callous exercise of age discrimination – the dismissal of individual workers as a result of their age.[6] The National Committee of Organised Labour on Old Age Pensions was founded in 1899. It campaigned for free universal state pensions for everyone over the age of 65, in order to combat the poverty created by the rejection of older workers by employers on the grounds of age. The work of Charles Booth on poverty in old age was particularly influential and Booth himself was a leading member of the campaign.

It was purely financial considerations that led Asquith to set eligibility for pensions at the arbitrary age of 70[7] even though 65 was the age used by most occupational and charitable pension schemes. The cost of the 1908 old age pension was further reduced by both lower and upper income limits, a satisfactory record of behaviour in relation to employment, and the maintenance of relatives. Those too poor to qualify for this pension were further discriminated against and left to poor relief.

The arrival of universal pension provision following the Second World War laid the foundation for age discrimination against all women aged 60 or over and men aged 65 or over. Beveridge's proposals were set out in a section of his report entitled 'The Problem of Age'. He built on the insurance principle established by the National Insurance Act, 1911, and the Widows, Orphans and Old Age Contributory Pensions Act, 1925, rather than the non-contributory means-tested model provided by the 1908 Act. This meant that pensions were not regarded as a right but were dependent on the establishment of eligibility through contributions or 'work-testing'.[8]

A second important condition proposed by Beveridge and put into practice by the introduction of the National Insurance pension in 1948 was the 'retirement condition'. Those who built up a right to a state pension by virtue of their contributions were only awarded the pension following formal retirement from employment.[9] Retirement and the receipt of a National Insurance pension were therefore tied together for 40 years until October 1989, when the earnings rule and the retirement condition were abolished.

In practice, however, the damage has been done. The retirement condition encouraged an end to workforce participation on a massive scale and established arbitrary ages as the customary retirement ages. Ironically, Beveridge actually hoped that a pension which reduced income and gave a higher pension to those who stayed at work, would encourage people to defer retirement: 'Making receipt of pension conditional on retirement is not intended to encourage or hasten retirement. On the contrary, the conditions governing pension should be such as to encourage every person who can go on working after reaching pensionable age, to go on working and to postpone retirement and the claiming of a pension.'

However, the universal retirement pension both encouraged and enabled employers to superannuate a whole section of the workforce on the basis of arbitrary age criteria. No move was ever made to introduce flexible or partial retirement which would allow older people to reduce the amount of work they did and to choose for *themselves* finally when to retire. As a result society at large has come to accept the devaluation of the economic role of 'older people' as defined by these ages. This has provided the main wellspring for widespread discrimination against older people.

What has this socially created discrimination against women over 60 and men over 65 meant to British pensioners? The major cost of age discrimination is economic dependency, the most extreme form of which is poverty. Of course poverty among older people predates retirement and this group have dominated the landscape of poverty since it was first described systematically.[10] But retirement and the retirement pension, while certainly providing subsistence incomes to prevent destitution, have created and perpetuated universal enforced unemployment among older people and the lowered incomes that go with it. Prior to the spread of retirement, workers were turfed out of their jobs on an individual basis across a range of different ages.

The latest official figures (for 1985) released by the Government show that just over 35 per cent of older people were living on incomes at or below the generally accepted Income Support (then Supplementary Benefit) poverty line, compared with 10 per cent of people under pension age. We know that in 1988/89 just over two million pensioners were receiving Income Support, but there are no figures for those living below or just above this poverty line. In 1985 some 60 per cent of older people were living in poverty or on the margins of poverty. This included over a million people living on incomes *below* the poverty line (a point I return to later). Moreover the long-term nature of retirement, unlike most unemployment, means that poverty in old age is an enduring experience. Thus older people predominate among long-term claimants: 75 per cent of people aged 60 and over have been receiving Income Support for three years or more, compared with 40 per cent of those under 60; elderly people comprise 60 per cent of those receiving this benefit for five years or more.[11]

In addition to poverty, the result of age discrimination is that pensioners are likely to experience low incomes compared with younger adults.[12] According to the DHSS, in 1982, only 10 per cent had an income above the average for working families and, at the same time, only 20 per cent of working families had incomes below the average pensioner income.[13] This high incidence of poverty and low incomes among pensioners is reflected in a wide range of measures of deprivation, such as lack of consumer durables, poor diet, insufficient heating and inadequate housing.[14]

The social security system is the main factor determining the living standards of the majority of older people. Over half of all pensioner income comes from social security.[15] The National Insurance pension is the most important component of social security provision and so the lower the incomes of pensioners, the greater the proportion the National Insurance pension comprises, and the less is derived from occupational pensions.[16]

Although Beveridge argued that once older people had worked a full course and fulfilled 'the obligation of service' they were to receive 'an adequate income to maintain them', this has never been the case in practice. Partly because of Treasury pressure to limit the overall cost of the scheme and partly due to ageist assumptions concerning the needs of older people, the National Insurance pension was set at a level of bare subsistence rather than adequate maintenance. For example, Beveridge allowed pensioners only 75 per cent of the scientific food value regarded as necessary for 'physical efficiency', in addition to 10 per cent for special food needs. The amounts required for clothing and housing were also set lower than those of a person of working age. Thus the definition of need in old age, which was adopted by Beveridge and was subsequently followed by all post-war Governments, was a minimalist one concerned with subsistence rather than the full participation of pensioners in society as equal citizens with other age groups. Not surprisingly, therefore, the single person's pension has remained at around just a fifth of average gross earnings over the whole of the post-war period. Furthermore the level of the state pension is low in both historical and international terms.

■ Comparative context

When pensions are compared to average incomes, post-war pensions are demonstrably lower than the relative values of those in existence in the mid-nineteenth century. Pensions then were equivalent to two-thirds or more of average incomes of working-class adults.[17]

The basic National Insurance pension is considerably lower in relation to earnings than those provided by most other European Community countries. For example, the single man's basic pension was 23 per cent of average earnings in 1980 compared with 41 per cent in the Netherlands, 36 per cent in West Germany and 32 per cent in France.[18] Reliable comparative statistics are hard to find but the European Commission has published some figures showing the relative purchasing power of pensions in each of the member states. Among the nine member countries in 1985 the British pension came second to last in what it enabled older people to buy in their own countries. In fact the purchasing power of a single person's pension in Britain was just less than 75 per cent of the French pension, 60 per cent of its West German counterpart and only 50 per cent of the value of the equivalent Dutch pension.[19]

There is also evidence that the economic effects of age discrimination are harsher in Britain than other comparable countries. For example, a major international study of seven Western industrial nations (including Canada, West Germany, Sweden and the United States) found that income differences between older people and those on average incomes were greatest in Britain. In 1980 the income of Britain's population aged over 75 was 67 per cent of the national average, compared with the other six nations where the income was 82 per cent of the national average.[20] Although income was more equally distributed among older people in Britain than in the other six nations, this emphasises the more universal impact of age discrimination in this country as well as its greater penalty.

In sum, mass retirement has been invented in twentieth-century society to exclude older people from paid employment at what are arbitary ages. Although the majority submit willingly to this process, very few of them have any choice in the matter. Thus the perceptions of older people themselves concerning old age, as well as the rest of society, have been affected by age-based retirement and pension policies. When accompanied by minimum subsistence pensions, as in Britain, retirement means economic dependency.[21] This does not mean that all pensioners live in poverty, but the effect of age discrimination is to depress the whole of this group's income and it is only those with access to higher incomes through, for example, substantial occupational pensions, who are able to cushion themselves against the economic consequences. Some groups also suffer the effects of additional discrimination on the grounds of race[22] and sex.[23]

▬ Discrimination within the social security system

The idea of the social security system discriminating *against* elderly people may, at first sight, seem puzzling to some other groups of claimants. For instance, the single person's National Insurance retirement pension in 1990 is worth 26 per cent more than unemployment benefit, whereas back in 1972 they were paid at the same rate and had been for most of the period since 1948. This suggests positive discrimination in favour of older people. But, in fact, it is conscious discrimination by policy makers against the unemployed which has had the side effect of making the relative position of pensioners look artificially advantageous.[24] In addition there are a number of ways in which the social security system directly discriminates against older people.

The latest available statistics show that in 1985/86 around one million people over pension age lived on incomes below the then Supplementary Benefit poverty line. This figure includes some 900,000 people who in 1985 failed to claim the benefits they were legally entitled to. This applied particularly to Supplementary Benefit, where 79 per cent of eligible elderly people claimed, compared with 86 per cent of the non-elderly.[25] There are various well-known reasons for this, including ignorance of benefits, convoluted claiming procedures and the stigma associated with means-testing. Partly for historical reasons, such as the impact the Poor Law made on their memories, and partly as a result of their attitudes towards financial 'dependence' on the state, there are grounds for believing that some of these factors are more acutely felt by older people than other age groups. Thus a social security system that includes a significant proportion of means-testing is bound to be age discriminatory in its effects. A strategy, such as the present Government's, of increasing the degree of means-testing or 'targeting' within the social security system is likely to deter even larger numbers of older people from claiming benefit, and so extend the age discrimination of the system.

Another major way in which the social security system discriminates on the grounds of age is in its failure to acknowledge disability among older people. This failure takes two main forms.[26] First, there is the absence of any official recognition that poverty is greater among disabled than non-disabled older people. Research has shown that older people with appreciable or severe disablement form a significantly higher proportion of those living in poverty or on its margins than older people with no disabilities.[27]

Second, there is the failure to provide for the fact that disabled older people require higher incomes than non-disabled people. This greater need is created, on the one hand, by the direct costs of disability – drugs, special diets, clothing, incontinence pads, handrails – and on the other hand, by the indirect costs. For example, there is the restricted access to cut-price supermarket shopping that many disabled older people suffer from. Because of their disability they are likely to be confined at home longer than non-disabled people, resulting in higher heating bills. Extra heating may also be required to offset pain, discomfort or poor circulation. Lack of mobility may mean that older people with disabilities have to incur the cost of private transport in order to get about.

The latest official evidence, from the surveys of disability by the Office of Population Censuses and Surveys (OPCS), revealed an average additional expenditure by pensioners with disabilities of £5.70 per week in 1985 and for the most severely disabled of £10.50 per week.[28] However, serious doubt has been cast on the methodology used to collect this data on extra costs, suggesting that it grossly underestimates the true costs.[29]

A consistent finding of both official and independent research is that the majority of people with disabilities are over retirement age. The latest official evidence shows that just under 70 per cent of adults with a disability – 4.2 million people – are over the age of 60, compared with 25 per cent of the general population. Nearly 20 per cent of people with disabilities are over the age of 80.[30] This does not mean however that the majority of older people are disabled: disability is not a natural and inevitable consequence of old age. The rate of disability for people over 60 is, in fact, only 355 per 1000 of the population and the rate for severe disability is much lower.

Because of the preponderance of older people among the disabled and the cost implications of recognising this fact within the social security system, policy makers have consistently tried to deny the existence of disability among this group, arguing that it is a 'normal' part of the ageing process. The latest official denial followed the publication of the first OPCS report in September 1988, when the Minister for the Disabled said that 'the resulting estimate of six million disabled people includes many who would not regard themselves as disabled or in need of special help from services or cash benefits. For example, almost 70 per cent of the six million were people aged 60 or over, many of whom consider the relatively minor limitations of hearing, vision or movement recorded by the survey as in fact normal for their age.'[31] The effect of this sort of denial of disability on ageist grounds is that older people with disabilities are among the most deprived groups dependent on social security.

It is sometimes argued that the additional costs of disability are offset, to some extent, by the more limited range of social activities they can engage in, which produces cost savings for them. However, this confuses effect with cause. It is the poverty suffered by pensioners with disabilities which forces them to change their behaviour. They often restrict their social activities because they cannot afford the services or assistance – including transport – which would help them to overcome the restrictions that disability imposes on their lives. Research shows that where older disabled people have high incomes they are not so restricted and are able to participate in activities – such as going on summer holidays and having evenings out – that are enjoyed by younger non-disabled people.[32]

The long-standing official denial of disability in old age means that the social security system does not cater for the extra needs faced by this group. When Beveridge addressed the different primary causes of need he distinguished what he saw as the 'problem' of age from the needs created by disability: the former being concerned with retirement from work as a result of age and the latter concerning the inability of a *person of working age* to work as a result of illness or accident.[33] Therefore the post-war social security system ignored the possibility of disability in old age from the very beginning. Since then, new benefits have been bolted on to Beveridge's structure and some of these have compounded the ageism of the system. Some examples will illustrate this point.

— Invalidity benefit
Older people with disabilities are not entitled to an invalidity benefit in addition to their retirement pension; they are either retired *or* they are incapacitated, not both. Men aged 60 and over and women aged 55 and over do not receive an invalidity allowance.

■ **Mobility allowance**

This benefit was introduced in 1976 with an upper age limit of 65. Although it was originally intended that entitlement to the allowance would cease at 65, the upper age limit for payment has been extended twice, most recently by the 1989 Social Security Act, when it was changed from 75 to 80. However, no one over the age of 66 who has not already claimed mobility allowance can now do so, even if they were unable to walk well before 65 and there is good cause for making a late claim.

■ **Severe disablement allowance**

This benefit, introduced in 1984, is intended for people incapable of work but with insufficient National Insurance contributions to qualify for sickness and invalidity benefits. The allowance cannot normally be paid for the first time after pension age because it is regarded as overlapping with the retirement pension.

■ **Industrial injury benefits**

Until 1987 this part of the social security system did not discriminate on grounds of age, the basic qualification being that an employee suffers disablement as a result of an accident arising out of and in the course of employment. However, the 1986 Social Security Act froze the reduced earnings allowance (previously called the special hardship allowance) on retirement and offset it against earnings-related pension, thereby reducing the compensation for the impact of disablement on those over retirement age.

■ **Board and lodging payments**

Nationally determined upper limits for board and lodging payments for physically disabled people in residential care homes are currently £60 higher than for older people. To qualify for the higher limit, disablement must occur before reaching pensionable age.

The age discriminatory aspect of disability benefits will be further worsened by the social security changes announced in January 1990 in *The Way Ahead*.[34] The expressed intention of the proposed changes is to give priority to those disabled from birth or in their early years. The neglect of the needs of those disabled after retirement age is excused by reference to the growth in pensioners' incomes in recent years which, of course, overlooks the acute poverty among older people with disabilities and the fact that the growth in incomes has been concentrated among better-off pensioners.

There are three significant proposals in the White Paper. First, a new disability allowance will be introduced for those whose disability begins before the age of 65. This new hybrid benefit subsumes attendance allowance and mobility allowance and creates a new lower level for each; this is in addition to the existing levels. The mobility allowance will still not be available to people over 65, though once awarded it will be paid regardless of age. (As a result of the age barrier those claiming attendance allowance after the age of 65 will not be entitled to the new *lower* rate.) Second, there will be age-related additions to severe disablement allowance, targeted at those who were disabled early in life. Third, a new disability employment credit for people of working age will serve to recognise a partial capacity for employment.[35]

The common outcome of these age discriminatory elements of the social security system is that two people with equally severe disabilities receive widely differing benefits and total incomes simply as a result of their age, and will continue to do so under the Government's recent proposals. There are a range of other anomalies in social security which particularly affect people with disabilities.[36] These inequalities may be illustrated with reference to the following imaginary case studies.

Inequalities in social security provision

Case A is an industrial injury claimant, first incapacitated under the age of 40.
Case B is a recipient of invalidity benefit, first incapacitated under the age of 40.
Case C is a retirement pensioner, first incapacitated after the age of 65.

Benefits (in £ per week)	Case A	Case B	Case C
Disablement pension	71.20		
Reduced earnings allowance	28.48		
Invalidity pension:			
Basic	43.60	43.60	
Invalidity allowance	9.20	9.20	
Retirement pension			43.60
Attendance allowance	57.00	34.90	34.90
Exceptionally severe disablement allowance	28.50		
Mobility allowance	24.40	24.40	
TOTAL	262.38	112.10	78.50

Notes: The figures refer only to benefits paid as of right and do not include means-tested benefits. The rates quoted are for a single person in 1989/90. The maximum rates of benefit payable have been quoted.

The anomalies revealed here are the direct result of ageist assumptions, which were built into the social security system at the outset and have been reinforced by successive governments. They indicate, in very crude terms, the value society places on disablement among people of different ages. Of course they not only reflect ageism in society but help to reinforce it and make it acceptable.

The Thatcher Government in particular has regarded older people as a *source* of income for redistribution to other poor and non-poor groups.[37] So, for example, the break in the earnings link for uprating the National Insurance pension in 1980 has resulted in cumulative savings of some £16,000 million. The Government has also gradually eroded the value of the state earnings-related pension through withdrawing the link to unemployment and invalidity benefit and reducing the income future pensioners will receive. Additional benefits for unemployment and invalidity have been cut, the ceiling on pensions for widows and widowers has been lowered and all contributors will eventually receive lower pensions than the Labour Government originally intended. Furthermore the present Government consciously targeted the incomes of older people for reductions, as the basis of its restructuring of the social security system in April 1988. The official estimate was that the changes would result in nearly half of those pensioners who were on benefit losing some income, excluding the reduced single payment entitlements. Subsequent evidence suggests that the proportion of losers may be even higher. For example, a small study in Scotland found that 89 per cent of pensioner couples had their benefits reduced.[38]

▬ Against age discrimination

Any proposals to tackle both the assumptions behind these recent policies and the long entrenched age discrimination within social security will have an uphill task. What measures are necessary?

In the first place, age discrimination in social security must be addressed as part of a general strategy against ageism rather than in isolation. It was argued earlier that mass retirement and the provision of subsistence pensions provided the wellspring for widespread discrimination against older people. Measures to promote more flexible forms of retirement – at a range of ages and on a part-time as well as full-time basis – and to outlaw age discriminatory employment and redundancy practices would therefore be an essential part of this strategy.

Second, social security itself must be overhauled. A recasting of the whole system, away from the Beveridge-style insurance base to the payment of benefits as a right of citizenship, would enable age discrimination to be abolished through the removal of 'need' categories, deriving from ageist assumptions. However, this may be regarded as a longer-term aim. In the short-term it is possible to begin to remove age discrimination by eradicating poverty in old age and age discriminatory practices within social security. A first step towards the abolition of poverty could be taken by restoring the earnings link for the uprating of National Insurance pensions abandoned in 1980 and the re-establishment of full entitlements to the state earnings-related pension cut in 1988. These measures would re-connect the living standards of older people with those of society as a whole, rather than allowing them to become more and more detached. Also, the gradual increase in the value of the basic pension in relation to average earnings is essential if we are to overcome the ageist assumption that older people have lesser needs than younger people. The aim should be to move away from a subsistence standard of income in social security towards one that allows older people to participate more fully in society.

As far as specific benefits are concerned, the removal of inequalities based on age would be technically a relatively simple matter. Mobility allowance, for example, could be extended to all older people who were eligible to claim it, but to do so requires an expression of political conviction that age discrimination is unjust.

Third, the major impact of disability on older people must be recognised within the social security system. The most effective means of doing this would be through the introduction of a comprehensive disability income scheme, which would allocate benefits according to the needs created by disability and would not discriminate on the basis of old age. The Disability Alliance has been proposing such a scheme for nearly two decades.[39] It would comprise a basic allowance to compensate for the restrictions imposed by disability, regardless of whether the person was employed or not, together with an income maintenance element – a pension paid when employment was interrupted or employment capacity was reduced partially by disability.

Age discrimination in retirement and social security are the main foundation on which discrimination against older people is based. Any progress towards the demolition of these foundations will help to promote a less ageist society and, therefore, one in which social justice for all older people can at last be achieved.

A BAD BUSINESS

AGE DISCRIMINATION AND THE CONSUMER

DAVID HOBMAN
David Hobman was the Director of Age Concern England for 16 years until 1987. He believes that discrimination against older people as consumers is yet another denial of choice in old age.

Recipient of the 1987 Rosemary Delbridge Award for advocacy, he now chairs the OFTEL Committee on the use of the telephone by elderly and disabled customers. He is also honorary consultant for Euro-Link Age.

In the mid-1970s a young woman went to a shop to rent a television set and was required to provide a guarantor. She gave the name of her father, who had recently retired with a substantial pension from a very senior appointment with a multi-national corporation. He owned his own large home and had plenty of capital. But his daughter was told by the assistant, 'We don't accept pensioners. They're no use as guarantors. Find someone else.'

So she did – her brother-in-law, a schoolteacher with a young growing family, a huge mortgage and debts all over the place. Unlike her father, he would have been useless if she had defaulted with her payments; but he was acceptable to the store.

Fifteen years later a man of 76, thinking he would like to try satellite television, collected the requisite number of newspaper coupons which would entitle him to a 30-day trial of a satellite dish. But when he came to trade them in and filled in his application, he was told he was beyond the age limit. The trial offer was to be followed by interest-free credit, if a purchase was subsequently made. The man wrote to the Home Office to enquire why laws against discrimination on the grounds of sex, race and religion did not also apply to age. The Home Office response was that age discrimination was not an offence under the Consumer Credit Act. So a pensioner was disappointed and the company lost a customer.

These two episodes confirm that discrimination is stupid as well as cruel. They also suggest that attitudes about the value of older people and their position in the marketplace may have changed very little. As in any other field, such discrimination is an unspoken attack upon people when they are categorised by some artificial common denominator: their age, their sex, their religion, their race or their colour. Even though it is known to exist, such discrimination is not easy to pin down and will always be denied when it is challenged.

Opinions about the value of legislation as a means of preventing this form of abuse are still divided. While some people believe discrimination can be outlawed and the Boards for Race Relations and Equal Opportunities have had some limited success, many would argue that the *malaise* is more likely to respond to public education because much of it is implicit in what people say and do.

As far as consumerism is concerned, discrimination against older people will only disappear as their cash flowing through the tills influences change. However, as the image of the older consumer as a pensioner on the poverty line has taken hold, the market had been slow to respond to the increasing affluence of older people.

■ Concessions

It is unfortunate that certain consumer terms reinforce the image of need and dependency. For example, the term 'concession', which is used widely in relation to the promotion of desirable benefits, implies a favour to a second-class citizen; whereas another term, such as 'off-peak tariff reduction', makes it clear that any resulting business is a bonus to the provider, as well as a benefit to the recipient.

Some concessions seem harmless enough, those which nobody minds and from which many people gain enjoyment; for example, reduced entrance fees for National Trust properties or Heritage sites. In other cases, concessions for cinemas, recreational facilities, hairdressers or restaurants may not be 'concessions' at all but devices to gain custom on days of the week, or at certain specified times when there would otherwise be little business. The widely used British Rail concessions for older people fill coaches during off-peak hours and throughout the special fare month, November – a month when fewer journeys are normally made.

Nevertheless, concessions undoubtedly create and perpetuate negative images of older consumers. Unfortunately, the consumers themselves and some of the organisations which represent them have fallen into the trap of confusing short-term expediencies with long-term solutions and now find that this focus on concessions may have actually distorted the argument for a decent income in later life. The cry should have been for *real* money, the only means by which genuine choice can be exercised and discrimination on the basis of age eliminated. The negative effect of such discrimination is illustrated by the practice in adult education establishments which treat pensioners as 'half persons'; colleges charge them half price for attending courses, but then insist that a class must have twice as many registrations as required for younger students, before it can go ahead. The result is that the class may not take place.

The older consumer, then, is seen as an object of charity. How far the concessionary nature of the market has resulted in a failure to explore the real and potential needs of older consumers is shown in a recent study of leisure opportunities. One theatre management which gave concessionary tickets, for instance, had never thought about the problems it caused its older customers by refusing advance booking and forcing them to queue for standby tickets. In another case, tea dances for older customers were interrupted during school holidays in order to give younger customers priority.[1]

As long as the market continues to see older people as objects of pity rather than profit, it will take limited steps to attract them as customers. Under these circumstances potential consumers will simply shrug their shoulders, walk away and do without goods they needed or wanted and for which they were ready to pay. If active steps are taken to attract the custom of older people, their response will reap its own rewards. At the same time, it will return a missing sense of dignity which citizens of all ages have a right to enjoy. Older people will be seen to be contributors to the prosperity of others, rather than a drain on national resources, as they are now often, wrongly, depicted.

Breaking the mould

There is nothing new in the notion that if discrimination was replaced with a better understanding of the needs of older consumers, it would reap its own rewards. Nearly 20 years ago, Age Concern England published its first report on older people and shopping.[2] The report's publication followed a conference at which it was estimated that older people were then spending upwards of £14 billion a year in the marketplace. The conference lamented the fact that manufacturers did not produce small packs of goods for single-person households, and that retailers paid little or no attention to the needs of consumers who were handicapped by age or poverty. The packaging of the goods then, as now, made them almost impossible for customers with stiff fingers to open.

One of the first people in the field to recognise the possibility of trading successfully with older customers was a Folkestone hotelier, Sidney De Haan. He was the founder of Saga holidays. He started his business at the lower end of the market by chartering whole trains and bringing Lancashire pensioners to small south coast hotels out of season, when they helped to retain key staff and keep the hotel doors open throughout the quiet months.

Saga travellers are now jetting around the world, but in spite of the company's undoubted success, as a 1989 report demonstrated there is little evidence that the British travel trade as a whole has fully understood the importance and increased spending power of the older and more prosperous customer.[3]

Holders of the purse strings

Times are changing and marketing agencies are now briefing their company-clients about the 'grey consumer', whose custom is becoming too valuable to be ignored. Conferences are held and expensive volumes of statistical information are produced to confirm this phenomenon. A conference in Paris in 1988 brought together marketing companies within the European Community to discuss this 'untapped goldmine'. The conference came to the conclusion that people aged over 50 now controlled half the discretionary spending money in Europe.[4]

This untapped goldmine, however, does not include everyone over 50. Rather, it refers to the 'Woopies' – Well-Off Older People – who are in their middle 50s, or at pre- or just retirement age.[5] These fortunate people are the first generation approaching retirement who have not suffered a significant interruption in their career because of the war. They may look forward to good occupational pension, a significant state earnings-related pension and a cash sum from maturing insurance policies. They may no longer have children to provide for. If they own their homes, they are likely to have little or no mortgage and some will have inherited property on the death of their parents. Some 150,000 homes changed hands in this way in 1988.

In the United Kingdom, savings are dominated by people over 50 years of age. The top third of this group accounts for 80 per cent of the market. Those aged over 55 now have a purchasing power of more than £25 billion annually, spending 13 per cent more than the average on holidays, cars and durables. Their disposable wealth is increasing faster than any other segment of the population.[6]

The prime target market, then, is seen to be pre-retirement. Surveys show that where the family head is aged between 55 and 64, more than the average is spent on home and leisure: 60 per cent more on home improvement, 38 per cent more on furnishings, 26 per cent more on cars and 17 per cent more on holidays. Manufacturers are encouraged to extend their range for this group who are also seen as an obvious growth area for alcohol, off-the-shelf medicines, hair colourants and restorers![7] Marketing agencies emphasise this age group's increased interest in leisure pursuits, for example in participative sport and travel. The Sports Council was quick to pick up an interest in this group in the early 1980s when they included people up to the age of 59 in their target groups to encourage increased participation in sporting activities. Even traditional banks are now developing marketing programmes directed exclusively at customers approaching retirement.

Such assiduous attention has never been directed at this market before. As a result, market intelligence is limited, and has led to contradictory stances being adopted by different companies. Some companies have entered the market with encouraging propositions, others not. Some insurance companies, for example, have offered competitive premiums to older drivers who have a clean driving record. Other insurers, however, have put a much higher loading on ageing drivers because of evidence which suggests that the risk of accident increases when drivers are in their 60s and over and fail to realise that their faculties are diminishing. In fact, once drivers are made aware of this they normally take compensatory action in their driving. Yet they can be refused insurance, while younger, less experienced drivers who are a similar risk, get cover as a matter of course.

The failure to properly research and understand older consumers is illustrated by several attempts to introduce promotions based on the American experience of discount-trading, linked to a magazine. In the United States, the American Association of Retired People is very successful, with a membership in excess of 30 millions. So far, similar attempts in the United Kingdom have not met their promoters' expectations. Not only have investors miscalculated the willingness of British people to join organisations – which may have been due to a lack of appreciation of the different cultures on each side of the Atlantic, disguised by a common language – but the benefits on offer through these so-called affinity schemes can be obtained in this country through countless other sources. Thorough market research would have uncovered this.

Several banks and insurance companies explored the possibility of creating locally-based groups of older people, linked through glossy magazines, but they withdrew at an early stage. This was partly because they were unsure about the outcome, partly because they were not able to segment the market with precision, and partly because the account executives in their advertising agencies, in common with many media directors, still appear to believe that prosperity is equated with youth. The habits of a short lifetime die hard. It is not usual to find brand managers or copywriters in advertising agencies who have passed their 40th birthday. This is bound to limit their vision.

▬ The image makers

The introduction of words such as 'Woopies', 'Wrinklies' and 'Golden Girls' suggests that the language of marketing is beginning to describe older people in its own terms. Such names will be distasteful to many older people, but perhaps their introduction is the prelude to recognition of other people's potential value and, in common with other caricatured portrayals, some of them are amusing or even helpful.

However, many of the distorting images of old age still persist. Advertisements seem to go from one extreme to the other. At one end of the spectrum they portray the nostalgic scene of silver-threaded couples drinking endless cups of tea, surrounded by cats, unfinished knitting, and unlit pipes on the mantlepiece. At the other end, advertisers find it difficult to admit that they are supposed to be addressing an audience in middle age and onwards. They avoid using any models aged over 50. A recent analysis of advertisements on London Weekend Television showed that less than 20 per cent included anyone who was identifiably over 55 years of age; only 5 per cent featured an older person in a major role.[8] These trends indicate how difficult it is for the market to translate what it has been told about the purchasing power of this group into reality.

At the same time companies are being advised to ignore the needs of those who are well into retirement. Marketing conferences which point to the sales potential of young-old people contrast them sharply with a view of older retired people as being on lower incomes and lacking an interest in consumption. Older retired people, they say, buy less food, spend less money on clothes, are not interested in modern electronics and take fewer holidays.[9] The result continues to be discrimination. The young old are brought within the pale and the rest are left outside; their needs are perceived as different and marginal to the mainstream development of goods and services.

Yet understanding where older customers fit in to the scheme of things is very important if discrimination is to be avoided, because it will influence both the products and the marketing approach. In its 1985 report[10] Age Concern stressed the importance of adopting a 'market viability' approach to older consumers rather than an approach based upon special needs. Older customers with special requirements do not wish to be seen as different. Their requirements may be similar to those of others, but at present the vast majority of goods and services on offer are only designed to be user-friendly for fit, athletic members of MENSA!

Design for living

Professor Bernard Isaacs of Birmingham University has said: 'If you design for the young, you exclude the old. Design for the old, and you include the young.'[11] His belief in the importance of getting the right products into the hands of older consumers led to the establishment in 1987 of a specialised consumer group known as the 'Thousand Elders'. Inspired by Professor Isaacs, the group was set up through the University of Birmingham, within the Department of Geriatric Medicine. Its underlying objective was to improve the man-made environment by testing a range of products.

A number of manufacturers showed an early interest in the group and among the first products it evaluated were alarm systems and home security ideas, doors and new types of door handles, windows, kitchens and bathroom fixtures.

If such ventures encourage better design for older people, they will undoubtedly banish practices which are unhelpful to most people, whatever their age: power points on skirting boards, washing machines which make you bend double to get the washing out, videorecorder cabinets which mean crawling around on the floor to put on tapes – all three are candidates for design improvements.

Discrimination and neglect has meant that the design of goods for older people remains a much neglected field, and questions about ease of access, the positioning of buttons and so on, have been much less interesting to designers than the aesthetic judgement. It was not until 1986, when the Helen Hamlyn Foundation staged an exhibition called 'New Design for Old' in the Boiler House at the Victoria and Albert Museum, that any major co-ordinated attempt was made to encourage designers to think about products for older people.

The objective of the exhibition was to encourage creative solutions to everyday obstacles and to replace what Helen Hamlyn, the founder of the Trust, called 'the sordid warehousing of our older people.' She called for much more effort to be made to provide an aesthetic environment where some sense of personal identity and dignity is preserved.

While the exhibition certainly illustrated ways in which fashion and furniture designers could create new products which were exciting, the tastes they displayed and, in the case of many items, the cost of the production would have removed them from the custom and purses of many older people. Inspirational leadership has to be followed by mass production and widescale distribution systems if the original ideas are to be successfully marketed. But manufacturers have first to be persuaded that a mass market exists.

Competitions for practical designs usually imply that prizewinning entries will find their way into the market, but in reality they often fail to find a manufacturer. This happened in 1990 to an imaginative device produced by a group of school children to help people change light bulbs without standing on steps.[12] This illustrates clearly the thinking of many manufacturers. If a product is perceived as being only for older disabled customers then it is not worth developing. In fact, easy ways of changing light bulbs would be welcomed by young and old alike.

Manufacturers should first distinguish what products would suit the market as a whole and then see whether any special requirements are needed by those who are very old. These special requirements rarely, if ever, jeopardise the suitability of the product for its main market. This kind of approach should end discrimination.

▬ Accessible goods in accessible environments

Making the appropriate product and ensuring it gets into the right hands are clearly critical elements in developing the market for older consumers. There are other barriers to be overcome, however, in terms of the purchase and accessibility of certain products. Widespread distrust of older people's ability to make their own decisions means that such decisions are often made by others. For example, it is usually necessary to have a doctor's certificate before obtaining a walking frame, and many physiotherapists would be horrified at the idea of older or disabled people actually helping themselves to such aids without the benefit of professional advice.

Yet, in this context, Professor Heinz Woolf of Brunel University has frequently discussed the use of what he would prefer to call 'tools for living' rather than 'aids for the handicapped', on the basis that customers should be able to purchase these items without having a disabled label attached to themselves.[13] Professor Woolf argues that an older person purchasing a walking frame in order to remain on his or her feet is no less natural than a parent purchasing something similar for an infant learning to walk. Both represent normal needs at different stages of life.

A welcome innovation in this field has been the production of a catalogue of equipment now issued by Boots the Chemists. The company displays goods, including pads for the management of continence, where they can be easily seen and purchased without embarrassment as part of the ordinary process of shopping.

Sometimes the only way to end discrimination against older people is to offer positive measures to suit their special needs. The eye's retina in someone aged over 65 captures about 30 per cent of the light of that in a 20-year-old.[14] This obviously has a bearing on the design of shop, type of advertising and form of packaging which will satisfy them. Informative labels and simple counter identification through symbols about the location of goods are of considerable help to older people, as they are for shoppers of all ages.

The Age Concern report on shopping,[15] which was produced in 1985 with the help of a group of representatives from major retailers, identified a range of environmental conditions which would be likely to attract older customers into stores. When asked about the factors which influenced how and where they shopped, many older people said they would be ready to pay a little more for their purchases at shops which provided places to sit down, had lavatories and employed staff members who had the time and inclination to help them. There was less interest in the possibility of home delivery, although mobile shops calling at the door would be an obvious service to housebound consumers. Developing a range of services for housebound people through collaboration between those who provide goods and services and local authorities would be a way to end discrimination against these most neglected of consumers.

A useful form of positive discrimination was introduced by some French municipalities when they decided to subsidise neighbourhood general shops. This decision was a clear recognition of the vital role such shops have as social institutions: they help to maintain the fabric of neighbourhood life, they make an economic contribution to the lives of poor people and they provide crucial human contact as part of an informal system of community care. Similar changes in British planning law to safeguard such shops would be a most welcome development. Undoubtedly, the human contact which shopping provides becomes increasingly important to people who suffer from social isolation. For them, there may be few regular callers apart from the men and women who deliver their post and their milk.

Sometimes older people do not use a service, because it does not suit their inclination or purse rather than because they have no access to it. Their use of supermarkets declines as they grow older. The shops which they visit most frequently are likely to be within about a mile of their home.[16] The distance they are prepared and able to travel will depend, of course, upon whether they are car owners or, if not, on public transport facilities. Since car ownership diminishes with age and since many older women cannot drive, a clear form of discrimination emerges in the sense that such people suffer restricted opportunities to travel and are less able to enjoy the benefit of greater choice and lower prices.

▬ New markets, new profits

The market concentrates on older consumers with the highest incomes, but there are nearly 15 million people over the age of 55 in the United Kingdom, and regrettably some of them are poor. But even poor people buy consumer goods. Perhaps because of their circumstances, they shop more carefully. Satisfying this apparently restricted market can yield useful profits, as Age Concern has shown through its low premium scheme for house contents insurance. This scheme started in the 1970s, in response to the demand from older people who were unable to find an insurance company offering adequate cover for the amount they wanted. The scheme now has a premium income of over £6 million a year.

Responding to the needs of people who live on their own – and some 36 per cent of people over 65 do – could increase sales on many items, notably food items, which rarely attract single householders because the goods are currently only available in large, wasteful quantities unless they are convenience foods. Only 40 per cent of this age group was reported as having a freezer in 1986, and the majority was therefore less able to store perishable goods. Offering small quantities would also give greater variety to people's diets, a variety which they may be unable to obtain if they can only buy in quantity.[17]

▬ Consumer protection

Consumers of all ages have a right to reasonable protection against the sale of faulty goods and, of course, against fraud. This is a right enshrined in common law and citizens' rights may actually be reduced by so-called guarantees which limit the redress which would otherwise be available. For their part, consumers should take reasonable care when making purchases; where there is small print it should be read carefully or, if it seems complex and the purchase involves a large sum of money, professional advice may be required. In this respect, older people's needs, duties and rights do not differ in any way from the rest of the population.

However, there are some products which are likely to be of particular interest to older people and some areas where mechanisms are needed to ensure they get a fair deal. Without this protection, particularly frail customers could be discriminated against and might be unable to counter the discrimination on their own behalf.

A need for adequate protection in the field of residential care, and to a lesser extent in relation to the provision of domiciliary services, has been advocated for some years. A report, issued in 1981 about the lives of older people and discharged hospital patients who live in boarding houses, led to the publication of a full list of the elements which should be enshrined in any code of practice.[18]

This has been followed by some authorities and voluntary agencies who developed codes, which they apply in relation to the homes which they administer. However, the system is by no means universally applied despite the existence of national guidelines and the sanctions against offenders are not nearly tough enough to deter all those whose standards are low or whose intentions in entering a profitable market are dishonourable. The system of inspection is still inadequate in many areas.

One field in which there has been misunderstanding, and which has attracted some adverse publicity, has been the provision of sheltered housing. In some cases, purchasers of leasehold properties have made assumptions about the level of service charges they would be required to pay which have subsequently turned out to seriously underestimate the increases which the manager has in fact levied over a number of years. As a result of this and other difficulties involved in the buying and selling of sheltered housing, the National House Building Council together with Age Concern and a number of major developers and management organisations, has worked out a code of conduct with which all new schemes registered with the NHBC must now comply.[19]

There may well be other areas of trading among older people where codes of practice can usefully be developed. Such codes should always be accompanied by sanctions for offenders, and must recognise that misunderstandings may well occur as a result of the purchaser's mistaken expectations, as well as by the failure on the part of the provider of the service or the manufacturer of the product to deliver.

There is, however, a danger here that older people will be infantilised when it is implied that they are no longer competent and able to discriminate for themselves. But if they fail to use the services of a professional adviser, or a properly equipped information centre, when there is small print to read and understand, they must accept personal responsibility if the terms of the agreement into which they entered, were unwise in the first place.

■ Chicken and egg

Looking towards the future, which has to come first? If we look to the example of shopping, will more convenient arrangements attract older customers? Or will older people themselves influence the marketplace through their purses, by only selecting those retailers and products which are user-friendly?

Many people today are becoming increasingly conscious of the environmental factors of consumerism and are limiting their purchases to those which will not damage the environment. They buy unleaded petrol, they buy aerosol sprays which do not contain damaging propellants and they boycott shops selling beef products which have involved the destruction of South American rainforests. The influence of these green consumers is apparent with the introduction of many new products and the demise of certain forms of packaging.

Can older people exert their corporate purchasing power in this fashion, or do their tastes vary to such an extent that they can never have this kind of combined approach? If this is not a practical reality, then any effort to counter discrimination against older consumers must come from the other side of the fence; from manufacturers of user-friendly products,[20] from retailers in the way they present goods for sale, and from those who are responsible for creating the environment in which shops trade.

If the process of shopping is seen to represent a leisure activity and a positive social experience, then the environment must be designed to make people feel comfortable. Consumers should not feel threatened. A great deal could be done with shop interiors in terms of the layout and presentation of goods. They should be designed to the highest mobility standards, making them easy and safe to move around in. Wide aisles should allow for the use of wheeled baskets or trolleys, and floor surfaces should be safe. Shops should be well lit. There should be seats and toilets within easy access. Lifts should be available. The solutions are often simple and nearly always self-evident.

While profitability remains the key factor in the use of expensive floor space, it would make sense to display the products which older people are likely to buy on the ground floor. This has been the case in libraries, where the Association of Assistant Librarians themselves came forward with policies they wanted to see implemented because they knew better than most how the arrangement of shelving, as well as the provision of good lighting, seating and magnifiers influences the amount libraries are used.[21]

These basic and reasonable requirements suggest that although new shopping centres will remain inaccessible to shoppers without direct access to transport, such centres may well prove more attractive to older customers than the traditional High Street. In a mixed economy, public authorities, developers, transport operators and traders all have their part to play.

In the final analysis, what is on offer has to be what older customers want. The people who manufacture and sell goods and services must want their custom and must understand its value. Ending discrimination against older consumers may be regarded as a moral imperative, but it also makes sound economic sense. It is bad business to ignore the older consumer, and doing so leaves everyone the poorer.

6 DEFENDING THE RIGHT TO WORK

AGE DISCRIMINATION IN EMPLOYMENT

FRANK LACZKO and
CHRIS PHILLIPSON

Frank Laczko, who is Senior Lecturer in Social Policy at Coventry Polytechnic, worked until recently on the second EC Anti-Poverty Programme. His interest in older workers began as a research student in Sweden in 1981. Since then he has been involved in two research projects on older workers, and has acted as a consultant to the Organisation for Economic Co-operation and Development on early retirement policies.

Chris Phillipson is Professor of Applied Social Studies and Social Gerontology at the University of Keele. He has been active as a researcher on retirement for more than 15 years. His initial concern was with the transition from work to retirement, and he has subsequently been involved in work on health education, notably the role of community care as it relates to older people.

Older workers in Britain have experienced conflicting pressures in the 1980s. In the early and middle part of the decade they were being urged to leave the workforce as soon as possible, as a way of coping with high unemployment and large numbers of school leavers. By the end of the 1980s, however, the position had been reversed, with calls on older workers to remain in employment for as long as possible. The *Sunday Times* reported that 'the elderly will be encouraged to stay in paid employment until they are 70 or even older.' Norman Fowler (then Secretary of State for Employment) was quoted as saying, 'We are challenging the whole concept that retirement ages should get earlier and earlier. It should be left to individuals to decide when to retire. . . . The present 60/65 fixed retirement ages are totally misconceived. . . . There is going to be much greater scope for people to continue in their careers for much longer, and greater value will be placed on their experience than ever before.'[1]

Much remains to be done to translate this statement into reality. In the 1980s older workers experienced great insecurity both in terms of holding on to their jobs and when searching for new work if unemployed. The purpose of this chapter is to examine in some detail the nature of age discrimination in the workplace. Our first step is to look at the context for the debate about age discrimination at work; in particular, the growth of retirement in general and early retirement more specifically.

▬ Retirement: the historical background

The emergence of retirement in the twentieth century reflects at least three important factors. First, as a number of studies have shown, retirement and the spread of pensions were stimulated by demands for greater efficiency and productivity in the workplace.[2] Second, the growth of the factory system helped to accelerate the process of retirement, with the development of assembly-line production hastening the displacement of older workers. Third, retirement has played an important role in periods of high unemployment. The idea of older workers being surplus to labour requirements has been crucial to the development of pensions both in Britain (the 1925 pensions legislation) and the United States (the Social Security Act of 1935). Similarly, the growth of unemployment in the 1970s and 1980s stimulated early retirement policies in a number of countries.

▬ Early retirement in the 1980s

In the late 1970s older workers, men especially, began to leave the workforce at increasingly early ages. Taking just the decade of the 1980s (see table below) we

Estimates and projections of the working population rates in Great Britain[3]
Men and women 45+

	GB workforce definitions			ILO/OECD* definitions		
	Estimates			Estimates		
	1980	1982	1984	1985	1987	1989
Men						
45-54	95.1	94.0	92.6	92.4	91.0	91.5
55-59	90.1	86.8	82.1	82.2	79.4	81.8
60-64	71.2	64.3	56.7	55.4	55.2	55.8
65-69	16.6	14.8	13.6	14.4	13.3	11.7
70 and over	6.3	5.9	5.5	5.2	4.6	5.2
Women						
45-54	67.6	68.1	69.2	69.5	70.8	70.8
55-59	53.6	52.0	51.1	52.1	53.0	53.6
60-64	22.4	21.9	21.3	18.9	19.2	21.0
65 and over	3.6	3.5	3.0	3.0	2.7	2.8

*ILO International Labour Organisation
OECD Organisation of Economic Co-operation and Development

find significant falls in economic activity for older men in all the age groups beyond 45. Indeed, by 1987, the rate of economic activity for men within five years of retirement was actually lower than for teenagers. Among women there was an increase in economic activity among the 45-54-year age group, but no increase among the 55-59-year age group, and a drop in activity among the 60-64-year-olds.

Although older men have certainly experienced a substantial decline in job opportunities, the problems faced by older women should not be under-estimated. Many find themselves in low-paid part-time employment, with few prospects for real security or advancement. Indeed, it is clear that there will need to be a significant improvement in the conditions associated with part-time work if this is to be seen as a real alternative for older workers. Job Start 50+ illustrates this point well; a government pilot scheme designed for part-time work only, it allowed people to earn a maximum of just £2.27 an hour in 1989.

Four main factors encouraged the decline in employment in the 1980s: first, the concentration of older workers, in many instances, in declining industries; second, the operation of particular schemes to promote worker redeployment (eg the Redundancy Payments Act) or replacement (the Job Release Scheme); third, the pressure of high unemployment; fourth, changing attitudes among government, business, trade unions and older people themselves, in respect of the older worker's right to employment in relation to other younger age groups.

The assumption of the Government in the 1980s was that the trend towards earlier retirement could be managed without new legislation to protect older workers from discrimination in the workplace. In reply to a parliamentary question in 1984, Peter Morrison (then a Minister of State for Employment) confirmed that 'the Government is not convinced that legislating against age discrimination in employment would be beneficial or practicable. We recognise the value of the experience, skill and other qualities that older workers bring to their jobs and we hope that employers will keep their employment practices under review.'[4]

The Government reiterate this argument when any attempts are made by individual members of both Houses of Parliament to propose measures to outlaw age discrimination. A further justification was added in a Department of Employment memorandum in 1988: 'There is currently no legislation in this country to prevent age discrimination in employment and the Government's view is that it would be neither beneficial nor practical to do so. Employers should be free to recruit the most suitable workers and not be restricted from doing so by legislation or regulation.'[5]

However, regardless of views about the benefits of legislation (and this remains, as we shall see, a matter of some controversy), the evidence in the 1980s was that simply leaving action to employers had left older workers in an exposed and vulnerable situation. Indeed, in many cases they were precisely the group targeted to carry the burden of job losses in the 1980s, and even when the economy improved they remained the group most likely to have long spells of unemployment.[6]

Age discrimination in the 1980s

It is easy to be complacent about the problems faced by older workers when looking for employment. The Department of Employment itself took the view in 1988 that evidence was lacking on the extent of age barriers in employment[7] and argued that the problems facing older workers would disappear as the demographic changes became better understood by employers.[8]

In fact, considerable evidence is available which shows that older workers face age discrimination in the labour market. What do we mean by the term 'age discrimination'? Age discrimination in the field of employment occurs when people are judged not by their ability to do a particular job but by their age. Such experiences often go unrecognised in the workplace. Workers, for example, are often quite ready to accept as final a statement that they are too old for a job, even when this is not the case. Indeed, we often find that older workers themselves believe that younger people have the greater right to a job, particularly in times of high unemployment. Age discrimination in employment can take many forms. It can occur when age is used as a criterion for redundancy or early retirement. It also occurs when people who want to go on working are forced to retire because of their age or because of stereotyped assumptions based on age.

Discrimination may be experienced both in a covert and an overt form. A subtle discrimination exists whereby a lower contribution is expected from older employees along with the view that 'the dynamic contribution comes from people under 35 and that the over-45s are, to some extent, passengers on the superannuation train.'[9] Such views are reinforced by the neglect of older people in areas such as education and training. A Department of Employment survey in 1988 of individuals attending courses or receiving job-related training, found that just 4.5 per cent of economically active men aged 50-59 and 1.9 per cent of those aged 60-64 had received some form of course or training in the four weeks prior to the interview.[10] Such neglect will also affect the attitude of the older employee:

a survey in 1989 found that nearly half of working adults aged over 35 could not foresee any circumstances leading them to undertake any further education or training.[11]

Older workers also experience more direct forms of discrimination. For example, a number of studies have indicated the extent to which age limits are set by employers. The most recent evidence comes from a survey by the Equal Opportunities Commission.[12] They monitored 11,373 job advertisements across a range of periodicals. Over 25 per cent of the adverts stated an age preference. Almost all specified the age of 45 or under; 65 per cent of the adverts mentioning age gave a limit of 35 or under. A study by MSL International analysed 928 advertised posts mentioning age, in sources such as the *Sunday Times, Daily Telegraph, Financial Times, Guardian* and various engineering publications. Of these adverts, 88.5 per cent mentioned an age limit of 40. A mere 2.5 per cent advertised for candidates over 46, while 9 per cent wanted people aged between 41 and 45.[13]

The Government have introduced some initiatives to stimulate the re-employment of older workers. For example, it abolished the earnings rule which inhibited some retired people from working because their state pension was affected if they earned over £75 a week. However, discrimination is still greatly in evidence in the various government employment services and agencies. These tend to be directed primarily towards younger workers and the short-term unemployed. Job creation and training schemes have tended to focus almost exclusively on younger people. The Employment Training Programme, set up in 1988 to help the long-term unemployed, gives a low priority to workers over the age of 54 who are regarded as non-mainstream (indeed those over 60 are not eligible to participate), even though it is older workers who are most at risk of experiencing long-term unemployment. Job Centres allow employers to put age limits in the vacancies they display and the Government will not stop this practice.

The British situation is mirrored throughout Europe where there is little evidence of government policy changes to encourage older workers to stay in work. France does have legislation against age definitions in job advertisements, but it is understood that this is not enforced in any way. Finally, despite statements about the importance of older workers, the Department of Employment have never carried out a specific study of the training needs of the over-50s.[14]

Stereotypes about older workers

Part of the problem that older people face when looking for employment is that advancing age is popularly associated with a declining capacity to work. A number of negative stereotypes continue to exist regarding the performance of older workers. In general, they tend to be regarded as less productive, less adaptable and less dynamic than younger workers. While there may be problems of productivity for a small category of workers, there is a substantial body of research which suggests that there is little foundation in reality for such views for the majority of occupations.[15] A great deal of research has been carried out with respect to the effects of ageing on physical and mental capacities. The main conclusion from this research is that although health and work ability decline in some respects with age, they are subject to considerable personal variance. Chronological age alone is a poor predictor of performance in a wide range of jobs. Research also suggests that individuals can adjust to, and offset, the changes affecting them in middle and later life. In a review of studies on productivity and ageing carried out in the 1950s and 1960s, one researcher concluded that 'productivity is, by and large, affected only minimally, if at all, by age.'[16]

Another common stereotype about older people is that they are too old to learn new skills. Older workers tend to be at a disadvantage when applying for jobs in today's labour market simply because they belong to a generation which had fewer years of schooling. They are at a relative disadvantage because individuals without any formal qualifications are more likely to experience unemployment.[17] As noted earlier, the lack of education and training of older workers is exacerbated by the unwillingness of government and employers to retrain older people. Employers are often not prepared to fund training for older workers. They believe that it is too expensive an option, given that older workers will remain in employment for a shorter period than younger ones. Moreover, there is also a belief that older workers are less adaptable and not prepared to retrain.

Where training programmes are geared to the needs of older workers it has been demonstrated that they can successfully acquire new skills. In a review of studies on the ability of the older worker to learn, going back as far as the 1920s, it was concluded that changes in learning ability with age are generally small.[18]

An ageing workforce

The issues discussed in this chapter have to be seen in the context of a workforce which is itself growing older. This means that more people will be vulnerable to age discrimination if employers do not change their policies. The structure of the labour force in Britain is undergoing radical change (see table below). There are now, for example, fewer young people leaving school. In 1993 there will be one million fewer 16-19-year-olds in the population than there were in 1983: a fall of 28 per cent. Numbers will increase gradually from the mid-1990s but by the turn of the century they will still be below current levels. In fact, people of working age will increasingly be concentrated in the middle age groups. In the year 2000 46 per cent of workers will be in the 35-54-year age group, compared to 40 per cent in 1988.[19]

The Ageing of the British Labour Force

ESTIMATES AND PROJECTIONS OF THE POPULATION OF WORKING AGE, GREAT BRITAIN, 1988 AND 2000

Source: National Economic Development Council (1989)

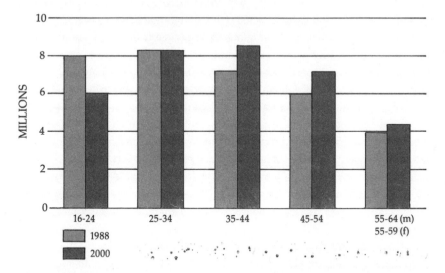

Some employers are beginning to respond to these demographic pressures by recruiting more older workers. Examples of such companies are supermarket stores such as Tesco and Sainsbury's, along with McDonalds, Thistle Hotels and Allied Dunbar. However, although these initiatives are welcome, they tend to be confined to 'non-standard' forms of employment and lower-paid jobs in the service sector. More important in the long run will be those organisations which have begun to change their career structure, thus enabling more older people to be employed or retrained to such employers as British Rail and Sussex Police.

Despite the examples given above, it is by no means certain that demographic changes will automatically lead employers to think again about their age discriminatory policies. First, many employers were until recently largely unaware of the changes taking place in the labour market. Second, pressure on older workers to leave the workforce early may continue despite the decline in the number of young workers. Enterprises have grown accustomed to using early retirement, not just to reduce headcount, but also to restructure their workforces. International evidence indicates that an early exit is not confined to declining industries alone.[20] This suggests that there will be a need for much greater government action if age discrimination is to be reduced.

Older workers and the law
Despite the problems faced by older workers, they receive no special protection or rights within the law. For example, an employer is not in breach of contract for sacking someone because of his or her age. Moreover, older workers lose the right to be protected from unfair dismissal if they are over the 'upper age limit' (this may be 65 or it may be whatever is the 'normal retiring age' for the job the individual holds). If, for example, the normal retiring age for a post is 60, those who are retained over this age may be discarded at any time by the employer.

In relation to redundancy practices, while it is not permissible for an employer to discriminate on the basis of race, sex or trade union activities, industrial tribunals have confirmed that it is acceptable for an employer to choose a worker near retirement age in preference to a younger employee. According to the Department of Employment, 'the Redundancy Payments Act of 1965 was designed to aid labour market flexibility and facilitate transfer between declining and growing sectors of industry. The size of the redundancy payment, with its age premium, may have encouraged some employers to shed older workers, the payments being seen as sufficient to sustain a period of unemployment which might last until retirement.'[21]

Mandatory retirement is not, of course, illegal under British employment protection law. Across occupations, pension ages vary arbitrarily and do not show any systematic relationship to individual skills or preferences. The consequences of an inflexible retirement age fell particularly hard on women as they have a lower pension age. Some women who started work after their children had grown up felt the need to continue working in order to obtain a reasonable pension on retirement, yet they were forced to retire at 60, because that is the age when they become entitled to a state and/or occupational pension. The House of Commons Social Services Committee acknowledged this in 1982, when it concluded its investigation of flexible retirement policies by recommending that the limit of employment protection for women should be 65.[22] This has now been achieved through the Employment Act 1989 because of a requirement in the second European Directive on equal treatment in occupational social security schemes.

▬ The American experience

Age discrimination seems to be a major feature of the British employment scene. Indeed, most European countries have tended to put pressure on older workers to retire in periods of high unemployment. On the question of training, a survey by the International Labour Organisation found that virtually no European country had a training policy focused on older workers. Moreover, with the exception of countries such as Japan, Canada and the United States, few public funds were targeted at retraining schemes for this age group.[23]

What of those countries with legislation which seeks to protect the older employee? How much difference has this made to their employment prospects? In 1967 in the United States the Age Discrimination in Employment Act (ADEA) was passed to protect older workers (aged 45-64) from a variety of discriminatory employment practices, including age-based discrimination in hiring and firing, providing employee benefits, and determining promotions, training and related areas. Amendments to the Act have now abolished mandatory retirement altogether for most categories of workers.

Clearly, this kind of legislation reflects a more positive stance towards older workers and their role in the labour market. However, it is important not to exaggerate the impact of the American legislation. First, the Act has made little progress in terms of reversing the trend in the United States towards earlier retirement. Second, age discrimination is still a major problem in the workplace. A survey of employers in 1981 suggested that most employers believed age discrimination was an admitted problem in many companies.[24] Third, a major obstacle limiting the effectiveness of the ADEA is the lack of awareness on the part of the American public that the statute even exists. Individuals need to be aware of their rights if this kind of legislation is to work. However, neither government nor employers may take the kind of initiatives that would increase awareness of age discrimination in the workplace.[25] Fourth, researchers argue that strategies aimed at protecting older workers, although increasing the job security of those who are in employment, may well intensify the problems of those who are unemployed. This is because the older workers' protected situation may make employers reluctant to hire them.[26]

Combating age discrimination: policies for change

There are now good economic as well as social reasons for tackling discrimination against older workers. Given the concentration of the workforce in the middle age groups, policies aimed at retaining these workers are an urgent priority.

Any proposals to alter the situation faced by older workers have to work at a number of levels: developing new social roles; using legislation to change attitudes; improving work prospects; raising income levels; increasing the effectiveness of health and social policies. Let us consider the key elements of any policy to combat age discrimination in employment. First and foremost, it is important to accept that a narrow employment-based focus is inadequate. The changes in work and the loss of jobs associated with new technology have to be tackled at a wider level. For older workers this means that trends towards early retirement are unlikely to be reversed despite shortages in some industrial sectors. The issue then is how to create viable social roles which maintain the status and security which people may have derived from employment. The agenda here suggests the need for radical changes to education and leisure, for expansion in outlets in voluntary work and for both economic and social recognition of the vital role played by older people within the family.[27]

Attitude change needs, however, to be promoted by government. Here, legislation may be important in terms of widening the opportunities available to older workers. The need for legislation has always been resisted by government and employers. But it may be important in terms of setting an agenda for change, for challenging stereotypes, and for highlighting particular areas of injustice faced by older workers. This has certainly been the view of groups which sought to draw attention to the problems of the long-term unemployed and older workers – notably the Unemployment Alliance in the 1980s and now the Campaign Against Age Discrimination in Employment (CAADE).

While it is important to press for legislation, we should also urge the Government to implement the recommendations of the all-party Commons Employment Committee. The committee recommended the following:
- There should be a bi-annual report to the Commons on the progress made towards achieving a decade of retirement between the ages of 60-70.

- The Employment Service should always ask employers seeking to impose age restrictions on recruitment if these are strictly necessary.
- The Government should mount a campaign with the Confederation of British Industry to encourage employers' awareness of the potential worth of older people and to challenge the practice of discrimination.
- The Government should review its own employees' retirement age and early pension entitlements to allow older people greater choice.
- A scheme the weekly earnings disregard from £15 for a man and dependent wife to £60 a week for six months, to encourage the over-50s to take on part-time work.
- Employment Training should be opened up to unemployed people over 50, irrespective of how long they have been out of work.
- A pilot scheme should give unemployed people aged over 55 £500 for an educational or training programme of their choice.[28]

Unfortunately, the Government still continue to repeat the view that it would be neither 'practical or beneficial' to introduce age discrimination legislation, and the majority of these recommendations have yet to be implemented, notably those relating to a bi-annual report, increasing the earnings disregard and improving employment training for the over-50s. It would still appear, therefore, that despite some initiatives jobs for older people remain a low priority.

One way of raising the profile of older workers might be to create a network of 'age discrimination officers' based in selected job centres throughout the country. They would be charged with specific tasks, such as monitoring discrimination, checking for ageism in job advertisements, creating a wider range of opportunities for older workers. Such posts would be funded by the Department of Employment but should have a consultative link with bodies such as local trades councils and chambers of commerce.

At the level of the workplace, support should be given to the section of the Institute of Personnel Management's code dealing with age discrimination. The Institute recommends the following:

- As a general rule, age should not be used as a primary discriminator in recruitment, selection, promotion and training decisions.
- Where age bars are used, the question should be asked 'are they necessary and why?'
- Organisations should consider incorporating in their equal opportunity statements their commitment not to discriminate arbitrarily on the grounds of age.

■ More should be done by organisations to provide counselling in career development and to encourage self-development for both younger and older employees.

■ Those responsible for in-house training programmes should recognise that older workers can still acquire and retain new knowledge and skills.[29]

At the same time, we believe that action on discrimination in the workplace must be related to broader questions affecting older workers. Among the most urgent of the issues that need to be tackled are the following:

■ Campaigns in the workplace must be launched to safeguard the rights of older workers. Attempts to coerce people into retiring must be resisted; rights to retraining must also be secured.

■ Opportunity should be provided for greater educational activity among those in later middle age, with wider access to college and university courses. Extensive retirement preparation schemes should be provided as a right to all workers.

■ Ways must be found to provide women with additional pension protection for the years of domestic responsibility when they are caring for children, handicapped or elderly relatives.

■ The problems faced by older workers must be used to develop a broad strategy to remove inequalities in working and safety conditions inside factories and offices. This must be related to the right for people to retire free from work-related injuries and illnesses.

■ The dependent status of older people must be challenged. This will require an attack on pension inequalities and social policies which stigmatise older people. Political and community structures must be changed to allow older people to participate on an equal basis with other age social groups.

■ Conclusion

Age discrimination in employment is a vital issue if wider aspects of ageism are to be tackled. Society itself is losing out when the skills possessed by older workers are ignored. Society loses even more when workers feel a loss in confidence and self-esteem following experiences of rejection when applying for jobs, a common feature of sustained periods of unemployment. We need therefore to consider policies which integrate older workers into society, either in terms of maintaining them in the workplace or facilitating options which develop new social roles which may or may not have a work element. We also need more radical policies to raise levels of income up to and beyond state retirement age. Periods of low income when workers are in their 50s and 60s can only mean a sustained period of poverty in old age itself. This is the ultimate consequence of age discrimination in employment. We urgently need new policies to challenge the insecurity and inequality faced by older workers.

YOUR COUNTRY DOESN'T NEED YOU!

AGE DISCRIMINATION AND VOLUNTARY SERVICE

DR ERIC MIDWINTER
Eric Midwinter is a social historian, educationist, consumer champion, author and broadcaster. Director of the Centre for Policy on Ageing since September 1980, his previous career was principally in the field of community education and the public service consumer movement.

He is Chairman of the London Regional Passengers' Committee and Chairman of the Health and Social Welfare Sector Programme Board of the Open University.

D o you find that letters marked 'private', 'confidential' and 'personal' are uniformly disappointing? They seldom mean the declaration of hitherto unknown passion; the long lost brother, thought vanished on an expedition down the Orinoco; the missive from the old-fashioned firm of solicitors, discreetly hinting at 'something to your advantage'. So I opened this one with practised diffidence . . . and, if it brought neither emotional nor financial reward, it caused me to dash off an angry – 'Disgusted, Centre for Policy on Ageing' – letter within the hour.

It was from an old pal of mine, an MP who had earned a splendid reputation as a devoted knowledgeable constituency member, not least because he had also been a councillor for years. Although urged by his party to remain, he thought, like a decent democrat, that it was time for someone else to have a go, and he retired at the time of the 1987 General Election. He contacted the Citizens Advice Bureau to offer his services, and down came the shutters. They take no one over 65, and retirement at 70 is obligatory.

The reply to my letter tamely confirmed this, explaining that it was considered wasteful and expensive to train anyone of that age, for their service would be too short. Reading between the lines, what they meant was that they were not going to train people who might keel over and die before the CAB had had its money's worth. I've just had a Christmas card from my old healthy friend; so that's two years' service they've lost for starters. Don't younger people move, have babies, and otherwise change direction? And this is advice we're talking about. It sounds, in my opinion, a rigid training scheme that can't accommodate the sort of previous experience that 70-year-olds have acquired. Sir Matt Busby is 70, but whose view on football would you prefer – his or one of those younger managers, all tracksuit and gold bangles? I am happy to say that the National Association of Citizens Advice Bureaux are currently reviewing this policy and are confident that the situation will improve.

Of course, people might point to the generals in the First World War and say, rightly, that they were a bunch of ancient Blimps. But I suspect that, because of their culture and background, they were also like that when they were young. During the Reagan presidency, the *Guardian* kept blaming his errors on age, and perforce, there I was again with another angry letter – 'Son of Disgusted, Centre for Policy on Ageing' – pointing out that, like it or not, Ronald Reagan had *always* been like that, making the same kind of statement and endorsing the same brand of policies. Age does not wither us: it accentuates our main characteristics.

More pertinently, age is not a helpful indicator. Yes, there are old fools, but there are also young fools, and vice versa. We must learn that age alone tells us very little. What we do know is that, in the United Kingdom, men who reach 60 have a further life expectancy of 16.8 years and women have a further life expectancy of 21.2 years.[1] We also know that there are over 3,000 centenarians now in Great Britain, compared with a couple of hundred or so in 1950. Yet retirement is still viewed as the beginning of the end, rather than, for many, the threshold to the last third of life.

The personal waste and the loss of all that resource of experience is as humanly catastrophic as the crashing of Brazilian rainforests, and it is on the same level of abandonment. It is extraordinary how little concern has been expressed about the effect of this attitude on the voluntary and civic sector.

Roughly, I combed through the library which is a fingertip from where I sit. It is the most comprehensive library on social gerontology in the country, with some 20,000 volumes, much unpublished material and in receipt of 200 journals. At first trawl, and, of course, that is not impeccable as an approach, there seems to be no reference to a direct and discrete book, chapter or article on age discrimination in the membership of or allied involvement in the voluntary and community sector.

Yet the examples of age discrimination are endless in the voluntary and civic sector. They advertise for people to present themselves as possible magistrates. But woe betide the culprit who trespasses on the wrong side of 50. The last advertisement I saw issued by the Lord Chancellor's Department stipulated that 'candidates must be below the age of 60 and preference is normally given to those under 50.' Half a life, apparently, is better than a full one.

Appointments to committees and councils

The Government appoints hundreds of people to voluntary bodies, quangos and committees of all kinds. Having been involved in a substantial amount of this sort of work for 15 years, I believe it is correct to aver that once a person reaches 60 there is an unwritten rule or convention which determines that he or she shall not receive a first appointment. I have been able, unofficially, to confirm this is the case. They might be re-appointed for a further term but, even then, anyone in his or her late 60s is unlikely to reign long.

Consider the folly of this. At exactly the juncture where one has probably completed the historic destiny of most humans – to wit, to have worked and to have raised a family – and one is contemplating, we hope, a constructive future, the door swings tightly shut. The retired person certainly has the time, often some apposite experience, and occasionally a little spare cash to bring to the cause. In many voluntary committees with which I have been connected, older people often (not always) offered a calibre of service that was admirable.

Yet there are places where they would not be welcome. The Department of Health's rules for Community Health Council Membership state that 'appointing bodies should not appoint people over the age of 70 unless there is a special reason: for example, an appointment by an organisation concerned mainly with elderly people.' One would hope there would be 'a special reason' for appointing people under 70, like they might be qualified to do the job.

When it came to structuring the District Health Authorities in the form which existed until 1990, the Department of Health stipulated that 'it is important to make appointments only where it is likely that prospective members will have the health and vigour to make an effective contribution throughout their term of office. Appointment or re-appointment over the age of 65 should be regarded as exceptional and should only be offered if equally suitable younger candidates are not available.'[2] That broad hint that 'health and vigour' are the prerogative of the under-65s, and the rather offensive recommendation that, given equal conditions, the chalice should be offered to the young are both blatant examples of age discrimination. Coming from the Health Department, who should know something about how difficult it is to align health and age, it really takes the biscuit.

So let's hear it for the Department of Education and Science. As long as they are aged 18, they don't care how old school governors are: what a pleasingly ironic relief to find schools, devoted to children, are more relaxed and progressive about old age than many other bodies.

That implicit decision to lock out a third of British adults from civic engagement is unethical. Officialdom, rightly, puts itself out finding representatives for and of women, ethnic minorities and disabled groups. Their anxiety if they cannot fill such a gap is close to laughable. Yet older people are either chopped or, worse, not given a chance.

So the call is for 'new blood'. You would think that a macabre form of nepotism had recruited hundreds of Count Dracula's descendents into the higher reaches of the Civil Service. One is constantly told that the difficulty is finding young people to join the voluntary ranks. This may be true to some extent, but let us examine the position arithmetically. For every ten British adults, roughly three are over 60.

One does not require all that many younger people, if equity is the watchword. I would like to urge acceptance of the Rule of Three in Ten. This stern law insists that, on any committee or board or council, there should be three people over sixty for every ten members. That is the demographic litmus-test.

An important issue to straighten out is the confusion between older age and length of service. It is true that many people cling to office, or are permitted to do so, and it is often that barnacle-like permanence which gives committees and boards a sense of dull sameness and an unwillingness to reform. Especially in the civic and voluntary field, the need to spread the responsibility and ensure others have their turn is or should be an essential feature of citizenship.

Let us, then, be clear about the difference between longevity of service and older people joining committees or boards as their first appointment. Older people are just as capable of providing new slants and ideas as anyone else. There is a very strong case for limiting periods of service in the voluntary sector, for it is frequently the irremovable elements which convey that wearying taint of backward-looking petrification. The anxiety is often more to do with getting rid of people who have exhausted their gifts, lost their way or, not unheard-of, should not have been appointed in the first place. The answer is not to fall back on the offensive utilisation of a harmless birthday, but to write into constitutions strict regulations about terms of appointment.

▬ How the 'old age' field feels

In 1989 Age Concern England sent out a questionnaire to institutional members of its Retirement Forum, its National Organisations Forum, and its own Age Concern Groups Forum. Three questions were asked about life and afterlife in the voluntary sector, and the response produced a strikingly confused portrait.[3]

One question related to statutory bodies, and whether there should be age limits on appointment and retirement. Although many responses were favourable, there were some unsatisfactory caveats. Several said firmly that suitability and fitness should be the only criteria, and that is fine, as far as it goes. But even these are a trifle accommodating: 'not on age alone' or 'provided that the member is still able to grasp and contribute to meetings' are riders that have an odd air about them. Why add them, with their evocation of the doddering loon, slumped, with listless ear-trumpet, over the board table? Should not that proviso apply to *anybody* serving on *any* committee? Is not the question more one of how we select and appoint committees in the first place? And these were the positive ones and, remember, they come from within the 'old age' field itself where, incidentally, two groups reported they had retirement ages for their own committees. Oh, dear.

Turning now to the representatives of old age who actually believe age is an *automatic* disqualifier, let us scrutinise the sorts of replies, among which this was typical: 'Capability should be the main criteria *(sic)*, but 70 years of age should be the limit.' Another response suggested the same limit: '70 – this allows recently retired people to use their experience but after this age their experience becomes dated.'

Several quote 70 as the upper age limit for voluntary and statutory committees and the like. The suggestion that experience has a 'sell-by date' is preposterous. It might be true of some forms of knowledge, but it is absolutely false in terms of experience. That apart, a strange phenomenon has occurred. Under the pressure of the age-discrimination lobby, people have half-learned the lesson, but they cannot bring themselves to believe in aptitude, rather than age. What they are now doing is compromising, in this half-baked manner, by raising the ante to 70. While everyone else goes about believing 60 or 65 to be the correct retirement age, those who pride themselves on being positive about age have lifted the chronological sights to 70.

This is a cop-out, and it is false on the counts both of principle and fact. One cannot meddle with discrimination. One cannot discriminate more or less. It is like those cases where women were, perhaps *are*, discriminated against because they were not 'strong' enough for a job or part of a job; but most people would prefer for such a task a strapping wench to a seven-stone male weakling, who gets the sand kicked into his eyes by the beach bully, courtesy of the Charles Atlas advert.

Even were the principle to be open to compromise, the inference that it is proper merely, so to say, to extend opening hours until 70 is itself based on a misconception about older age – and one is unhappy to note its manifestation among a clutch of answers from old-age-oriented agencies. There is a popular view that the rise in the proportion of older people in our society is the consequence of 'longevity', of people living longer. That is not strictly true. Indeed, the chief reason why the *proportion* of older people is so large is because the *proportion* of younger people is so much smaller, having this century almost halved, while the former has trebled. But, in so far as older age itself is concerned, it is a question of survival, rather than the species existing longer. In other words, more people are surviving to 60, and enjoying the kind of lifespan which has never been all that rare, but which is now much more common, simply because so few humans die at or just after birth, in the first five years of life, and so on.

Thus the notion that being 70 is qualitatively different from being 70 in centuries past, assuming comparable social circumstances, is imprecise. All praise, therefore, to the organisation which answered, squarely and purely: 'Age limits are unfair.'

When the same question about age limits was addressed in terms of voluntary agencies rather than statutory bodies, it was interesting to observe that there was less tension in the answers. The respondents were most relaxed about volunteers. While they might wish GPs and JPs to retire automatically at 70, not so hard a front was forthcoming apropos volunteers. One interpretation must be that voluntary work is viewed as rather less significant, in the sense that some old person doing a little forest conservation is less likely to be as dangerous as the ancient quack prescribing cupping or the antiquated magistrate consigning culprits to the stocks.

But, once more, the qualifications were liberally added: 'as long as the individual is active and capable of carrying out the required duties'; and 'where risks to other persons are involved (eg driving), then adequate checks on ability should be made.' Again, symptoms are confused with problems. Would you retain a 20-year-old Mr Magoo as your chauffeur?

What we see is a fleeing away from the central issue of judgement and assessment. When the Civil Service proceeded to the first comprehensive retirement programme in the 1850s, the justification for imposing the cowardly administrative convenience of an age barrier was how invidious it would have been to attempt any form of assessment. The unspoken thought appears to be, if you don't have an age barrier, volunteers will persist willy-nilly, without any let or hindrance.

What age discrimination provides is a workable, but unethical and wasteful measure. What is necessary is its replacement by formats of review and assessment including, if appropriate, medical and physical tests, but irrespective of age. The feminist parallel is again evident: it was all too easy to have massive walls built against women in practically every walk of life. As they were demolished, more refined and juster modes of recruitment, selection and assessment had to be developed. Whether for statutory or voluntary appointments and bodies, the abandonment of another gross inequity – to wit, ageism – requires a more sophisticated set of judgements.

A third question was posed in Age Concern England's questionnaire, asking for examples of discrimination. Apart from those previously quoted there were other instances mentioned of retirement conditions: county and local WRVS posts of responsibility: 65; guiding and scouting in uniform: 65; British Red Cross volunteers: 75; St John's Ambulance Brigade: no new volunteers of 65 or more, and volunteers over 65 need an annual medical and fitness certificate up to 68, although this might be extended to 70; lay magistrates on the Juvenile panel: 65, others 70; Industrial Tribunals: chairmen 72, members 68. 68? What does that really mean? What is so significant about 68? How was that rationally decided upon? Imagine the song: 'He's 68 today, 68 today; He's lost the key of the door . . .' It has neither official nor cultural usage behind it.

Of the others – and this is no more than reportage of answers to the question – the ambulance services emerge reasonably well, in that they allow service by right of assessment. Even then, I would have been happier if all my St John's and Red Cross personnel were proved medically fit. In the mind's ear, one hears the patient cry: 'Send for some 66-year-old ambulancemen and women: they're the only ones certified as healthy.'

Organisations sometimes have age discrimination thrust upon them by the vicissitudes of insurance. Over and again, one hears the complaint that, for some tasks, insurers have exclusion clauses according to this or that age limit. The Volunteer Centre tell us: 'We are beginning to do some work in this area to change this practice', and our best wishes go out to that august body.

In practical terms, the replacement theory could well be utilised: it would seem useless to go to the insurance companies merely waving a banner or principle; if methods of assessment, such as medical tests, were introduced, insurers might find them more acceptable.

■ Jury service: a case study

A valuable case study of this whole argument is the matter of jury service. On old-style electoral registration forms it told the form-filler to put a tick in a particular column if the person listed were over 65, for they were ineligible for jury service, it quoted baldly and starkly, 'on grounds of age'. The Centre for Policy on Ageing campaigned heartily about this, arguing that this ancient, centuries-old right, steeped in Anglo-Saxon tradition, should not be denied a quarter of the nation's adult citizenry. It was ageist and an illustration of rendering older people second-class citizens, denying them involvement in a previous freedom many had fought to sustain. Here was a long-established bastion of English liberty, older than the vote, yet older people were banished from participation. There wasn't a dry eye in the house.

The first official communiqué in answer to this stirring cry from the battlements was the predictable triple jump of bureaucrats: it is illegal; it is impractical; it is expensive. Some months later, they relented, thought twice, listened to some extra argument about how every jury is skewed in that two or three of its number are not over 65, and, as such, does not express itself as a cross-section of the populace. As a result of this and other lobbying, the Criminal Justice Act 1988 proclaimed that jury service would be extended to 70, but as we suggested, those between 65 and 70 may decline, if they wish. This was implemented as from 19 February 1990.

There is a tiny case study within a case study. Although we would urge a total abandonment of an age limitation, those of us wearied by years of banging heads against, not so much the walls, as the balloons of officialdom (for, eventually, walls splinter a trifle, whereas ballons bulge inwards and then return to their old shape), understand that we must count our blessings in small twopenny-pockets. We regarded this as a minor success, for it is a step in the right direction, an interim success. That is why it is different from insisting, for instance, on retirement from voluntary service at 70. That is a declared policy – and it is wrong. The equivalent of our restrained glee over this little triumph is an organisation whose policy is: we will use people of any age . . . but those bastards at the insurance company won't let us use anyone over 70.

But what was very enthralling about the jury service argument was the effect it had on older people themselves. Many, it is true, shouted enthusiastically that we were right and to be congratulated, but many others were up in arms at our intrepid temerity. I recall a debate at an Age Concern England governors' meeting no less when, in answer to my piping treble advocating such a reform, there were those present who urged caution, on the grounds that old people became blinder, deafer and dafter (to be fair, 'couldn't take in things so quickly' and 'couldn't concentrate as much' were the euphemisms actually employed). Back, back we find ourselves in the frustrating and confusing conceptual warp. Of course, there are many older people whose eyesight or hearing is failing or who can't concentrate as assiduously. No one pretends that ageing has no ill-effects: the argument is that birthdays do not signpost them. If one has poor eyesight or hearing at a younger age, then an appeal against jury service is likely to be upheld. But why that sweeping obliteration of an entire generation because some may be incommoded?

The mailbag and telephone line brought many criticisms. One gentleman said that on his 65th birthday his sole thought had been, not the hope that his grandchildren would send a card, but that never again would the manilla envelope summoning him to do jury service tumble through his letterbox. He had done jury service four times: but surely that is another problem. There would seem to be a strong argument, with so many millions of us, only to do it once. Others spoke of the dread of being assaulted by bellicose friends of the accused, or of retirement meaning putting up your feet forever. One person informed us that he lost four and a half stone doing jury service: we considered sending on his letter to weight-watchers, so that the future courtroom might feature twelve fat men and true.

Thus there were plenty of Henry Fonda's 'angry men' outside the jury room, but most of their complaints were not age-related. What the exercise revealed was that ageism is a phenomenon shared and indulged by older people themselves. It is hardly to be expected that it would be otherwise. Old people have been indoctrinated for so long in the necessary frailty and peripheralism of their lot that this is not surprising. Part of the campaign against any form of discrimination has this problem: part of the success of any such campaign carries with it, by the yardstick of some, disbenefits. Older people are delighted when organisations urge that pensions should be increased, so that pensioners might be 'first-class citizens'. Being a first-class citizen, however, has responsibilities as well as rights. Doing jury service could be one of them. Being a first-class citizen is about that kind of civic engagement.

■ Ageism as a lifelong concept

For older people to have the opportunity to participate not only on juries but in other civic activities after they retire, the major proposals must be:

— the end of any age discrimination for voluntary participation in the statutory and the voluntary sectors, especially and initially from those bodies who have it within their own control so to devise and endorse;

— the promotion of the Rule of Three in Ten as a rule of thumb for all organisations in the formation of committees, boards and the like;

— the establishment of forms of fixed terms of appointment, assessment, review etc which obviate the need to use age as a convenient tool;

— the continuance of the pressure on insurers to change their practice.

Finally, there is a contextual issue, briefly dealt with, but of supreme importance. Age discrimination is not old age discrimination. It is about the false use of personal chronology as an indicator or touchstone of human capacity and worth. If it is misleading to sack magistrates at 70, it is misleading to have a school-starting age of five or driving licences available at 17. Although that is not immediately relevant to this essay, it should, nonetheless, be always remembered. The only advantage of birthdays is getting presents and, even there, we might follow the example of one or two cultures, and have them all on the same day. Age intervenes, like religion, gender and ethnicity and other discriminators, in the decent, even-handed and civilised passage of human relationships.

POSTSCRIPT
WHAT DO YOU THINK?

A newly retired further education teacher who had worked for both the Home Office as a prison instructor and for a local authority as a teacher of technical subjects, applied for two part-time jobs. The first was six hours a week teaching YTS students, the second was with the probation service supervising community service work at the weekends. In both cases the interviewers wanted to appoint him but they were told they could not by their authorities. He was 65 years old.

This story was taken from the experiences of members of organisations on Age Concern's governing body[1]. It was the most glaring example of the arbitrary choice of any particular chronological age – in fact one moment in time – to exclude people from participation, services or benefits. But there were many others. People were refused regular blood pressure testing because they were 65, they could not obtain a mobility allowance following an accident which occurred when they were 65, they were not welcomed by voluntary agencies who – one would imagine – are crying out for workers. They were even prevented from giving blood to help keep others alive.

The authors in this book are unanimous: a date at which we all become 'aged' is nonsense. Older people are not an homogeneous group distinguished by frailty, lack of sense and dependency. The years of retirement can span more years than some people spend in paid work. Just as a 16-year-old is different from a 50-year-old, so a 50-year-old will differ from a 90-year-old . . . and each individual will be different from another.

Ageism is embedded in our attitudes and social structures. It can even be encountered by younger people – as a glance at job advertisements will show. We treat older people as a group and set them at the margins of society. Although the authors in this book agree that the situation is iniquitous, they differ in their views of the solution. Some favour legislation, Steve Scrutton going so far as to argue that the general term 'age' should never be used in legislation as a shorthand term to denote frailty or dependence. Some present detailed programmes for change which will require legislation, for instance, legislation to improve the levels of pension and older people's access to employment. Others draw back from legislation and look to a change in attitudes on the part of professionals and employers. David Hobman, however, is more sceptical of this view in relation to the consumer: 'It is their cash flowing through the tills which will influence change.' Older people must be able to take matters into their own hands.

Several authors look hopefully towards the emergence of a grey power movement in Britain to counter the ageism which, as Steve Scrutton shows, has been endemic in Western civilisation throughout its history and is evident in other cultures. In the late twentieth century compulsory retirement has depressed social status, a point also made by Alan Walker, and has led to medical, educational and social service provision receiving a low priority because it gives a low marginal rate of return on investment. Steve Scrutton considers legislation essential in many areas.

Mary Marshall explores the ways in which the attitudes of professional workers and even older people themselves reveal a poor image of old age. This is not surprising when one considers the ways in which the attitudes and structures of society condition us from the early years of life. She also points to the danger of a new tendency to give attention to affluent active newly-retired people, which only serves to concentrate ageism on older, poorer people. She believes we must all recognise and come to terms with our own ageism and seek to break down the barriers to understanding. In this, the media – particularly television – could play a major role.

Mary Marshall recommends that:

■ each profession includes an anti-ageist statement in its code of conduct, as the National Union of Journalists has done;

■ older people are involved as fellow students and teachers in schools;

■ older people help make the decisions in their own communities and, if they live in institutions, in how these are run;

■ older people have a role in training health and social care professionals.

Melanie Henwood in her chapter on healthcare emphasises that old age itself is not a disease and that many of the conditions associated with it are neither inevitable or universal. Physiological change affects everyone, but the degree of change is very wide ranging and there is considerable variation between individuals.

For healthcare to be non-discriminatory we must ensure that:

■ prevention and treatment of chronic disease is given priority, with an acknowledgement of the important role played by speech, physio and occupational therapists, chiropodists and hearing technicians in maintaining an acceptable quality of life for those with chronic conditions;

- critical questions are asked about the volume and quality of health services for older people compared with those provided for younger groups;
- purely economic approches to healthcare provision are balanced by humanitarian and ethical considerations which value the lives and well-being of older people;
- urgent attention is given to offering screening for, and treatment of, osteoporosis;
- the exclusion of older people from screening and treatment programmes is not arbitrary;
- structural changes to the social and health services brought about by the NHS and Community Care Act and changes to GP contracts are monitored to ensure that they do not adversely affect older people;
- the importance of geriatricians and psychogeriatricians in the care of older people is reflected in local health plans;
- there is more research into the normal processes of ageing and that longitudinal studies are developed.

Alan Walker argues that the social security policies have played a central role in putting people on the margins of society, forcing them into retirement and then providing them with a pension which reduces many older people to economic dependency and even poverty. Britain compares unfavourably with other industrial nations in the extent to which its older citizens are forced to seek assistance through intrinsically discriminatory means tested benefits. Double discrimination is experienced by older disabled people whose needs are not acknowledged and who are denied access to benefits available to younger people.

Alan Walker argues that the income of retired people must be raised and he sets out a series of specific measures to:

- restore the earnings link for state pensions;
- re-establish the original entitlements within the State Earnings Related Pension;
- make the mobility allowance available to everybody whatever their age, if they qualify on the grounds of disability;
- introduce a comprehensive disability income scheme, which would give an income to those who could not work, or whose work was interrupted or restricted by disability. There would also be an allowance to cover the additional expenses which disability inevitably incurs.

In order to stop the position deteriorating further, Alan Walker also argues that changes to social security should be monitored closely to prevent further age discrimination through cuts in benefit, which disproportionally affect older people.

David Hobman relates how discrimination against older people in the market for goods and services shows little sign of waning, apart from the new concentration on the commercial potential of selling to the affluent pre-retired. He argues that older people harm their own status by demands for concessions which reinforce notions of dependency and detract from the campaign for an adequate income. He believes that:

■ companies should consider the needs of older customers when designing goods, facilities and services;

■ aids for the disabled should be readily available and regarded as acceptable tools for daily living;

■ enforceable codes of conduct should be developed to protect vulnerable consumers.

Frank Laczko and Chris Phillipson show how the emergence of retirement in the twentieth century created a sharp dividing line between those who were seen to be actively part of the community and those who were not. Unemployment in the 1980s forced many older people into early retirement and made it difficult for others to find work. Their chapter includes recommendations from the Institute of Personnel Management and the House of Commons Employment Committee which are designed to improve the situation of older people in employment and on moving into retirement. For instance, the Institute of Personnel Management proposes that organisations should consider including a commitment not to discriminate arbitrarily on the grounds of age in their equal opportunities policies. The House of Commons Employment Committee proposes the establishment of a 'decade of retirement' between the age of 60 and 70, which would allow people to choose for themselves when they wished to retire over this period of time.

Laczko and Phillipson do not suggest following the course taken by the United States and introducing an Age Discrimination in Employment Act, but they are convinced that it is important to press for legislation as well as seeking to improve the attitudes of employers. They argue that:

■ there should be a network of age discrimination officers, placed in job centres, to improve job opportunities for older workers;

■ attempts to coerce people to retire must be resisted and rights to training secured;

■ working conditions should ensure that people can retire free from

work-related illnesses;
- higher levels of income should be ensured for older workers;
- a way should be found to give women additional pension cover for years of domestic responsibility;
- attention should not only focus on the workplace. People naturally want to retire and it is therefore important to offer opportunities for fulfilment in leisure, education and voluntary activities and to recognise the valuable role played by older people within the family.

Eric Midwinter is quite categoric in his chapter about the discrimination which exists against older people in government appointments to voluntary office and which is applied by voluntary organisations themselves towards their older volunteers. He reveals the ambivalent attitudes at the heart of the Age Concern movement, and describes as a 'cop out' the proposal to raise the age limit of office from 65 to 70. One cannot, he says, discriminate more or less.

He believes that older people should be given the opportunity to participate in civic activities during retirement and argues for:
- the end of any age discrimination for voluntary participation in the statutory and voluntary sectors, especially and initially from those bodies who have it within their own control to do so;
- the promotion of the Rule of Three in Ten; that is, that in any group of ten people a rule of thumb for all organisations in the formation of on committees, boards and the like – three should be aged over 60;
- the establishment of fixed terms of appointment, assessment, review etc which obviate the need to use age as a predetermined limit;
- continued pressure on insurers to change their practice of imposing exclusion clauses on arbitrary age limits.

The authors propose two ways forward: they encourage a change in attitudes and they call for some specific legislative measures. Both courses of action might be assisted by an Age Discrimination Act which would become the benchmark for policy and practice. It could follow the lines of the Sex Discrimination Act 1975 and the Race Relations Act 1976 in making age discrimination 'unlawful in employment, training and related matters, in education, in the provision of goods, facilities and services and in the disposal and management of premises. [2, 3] Such legislation gives individuals the right of direct access to the civil courts and industrial tribunals for legal remedies for unlawful discrimination. Such an act could be accompanied by a Commission against Age Discrimination both to help enforce the legislation and promote equal opportunities for people regardless of age.

Some people will argue that this is the only way to achieve any measure of success, others will discount the idea as absurd. If you have read this far, and have contemplated the examples of discrimination which are quoted, then join the debate: do not dismiss the problem.

Over 30 years ago J H Sheldon, whose *'Social Medicine of Old Age'* is still one of the most farsighted and compassionate reviews of the circumstances of older people, described old age as 'a quality of mind and body whose time or onset varies from individual to individual, rather than a mere quantity expressed by the term of duration applicable to all.'[4] If we deny this, surely we deny profit to society, opportunity for today's older people and hope for our future selves.

EVELYN McEWEN
Divisional Director, Services
Age Concern England

REFERENCES

1 AGEISM: THE FOUNDATION OF AGE DISCRIMINATION

1 Greengross, W and S (1989) *Living, Loving and Ageing,* Age Concern England, London.
2 Minois, G (1989) (also reference 9) *The History of Old Age: From Antiquity to the Renaissance,* Polity Press/Blackwell, Oxford .
3 Office of Population Censuses and Surveys (1901-1981 census data). Population projections by the Government Actuary (1987-2027), pp2, no 16, HMSO, London.
4 Ory, M and Bond, K (eds) (1989) *Ageing and Health Care: Social Science and Policy Perspective,* Routledge, London.
5 Tyler, W (1986) (also reference 7) Structural Ageism as a Phenomenon in British Society. *Journal of Education Gerontology,* Keele.
6 *As You Like It* (II, vii).
7 Tyler, W (1986) (reference 5).
8 Freud, S (1905) *On Psychotherapy,* Hogarth Press, London.
9 Minois, G (1989) (reference 2).
10 Townsend, P (1981) (also reference 16) The Structural Dependency of the Elderly: A Creation of Social Policy in the 20th Century. *Ageing and Society,* 1, 6-28, London.
Phillipson, C (1982) (also reference 16) *Capitalism and the construction of Old Age,* Macmillan, London.
Myles, J (1984) *Old Age in the Welfare State: the Political Economy of Public Pensions,* Little/Brown, Boston.
Phillipson, C and Walker, A (1987) *Ageing and Social Policy: A Critical Assessment,* Gower, Aldershot.
11 Evandrou, M and Falkingham, J (1989) Benefit Discrimination, *Community Care,* 25 May.
12 Scrutton, S (1989) Time to Treat Elderly People Like Children? *Social Work Today,* 10 August, Birmingham.
13 Eastman, M (1984) *Old Age Abuse,* Age Concern England, London.
14 Levin, J and Levin, W C (1980) *Ageism: Prejudice and Discrimination Against the Elderly,* Wadsworth, Belmont, California.
15 Cummings, E and Henry, W E (1961) *Growing Old: the Process of Disengagement,* Basic Books, New York.
16 Townsend, P (1981) (reference 10). Phillipson, C (1982) (reference 10).
17 Norman, A (1987) *Aspects of Ageism: A Discussion Paper,* Centre for Policy on Ageing, London.
18 Norman, A (1985) *Triple Jeopardy: Growing Old in a Second Homeland,* Centre for Policy on Ageing, London.
19 Age Concern England (1989) Retirement Forum: Responses to Questionnaire (unpublished).
20 Beauvoir, S de (1972) *Old Age,* Deutsch/Weidenfeld and Nicholson, London.
21 Scrutton, S (1989) *Counselling Older People: A Creative Response to Ageing,* Age Concern England/Edward Arnold, London.
22 Gore, Irene (1979) *Age and Vitality,* Allen and Unwin, London.

2 PROUD TO BE OLD: ATTITUDES TO AGE AND AGEING

1 Sidhartha Films Ltd (1984) *The Elderly,* a survey conducted by Social Surveys (Gallup Poll) Ltd, London.
2 Gibbs, N R (1988) Grays on the Go. *Time,* 22 February, New York.
3 Marris, P (1979) *Loss and Change,* Routledge & Kegan Paul, London.
4 Parkes, J M (1975) *Bereavement: Studies of Grief in Adult Life,* Penguin Books, London.
5 Eastham, E A (1989) The Ageing Notion: A Problem for Society or Created by Society? *Health Visitor,* 58, London.
6 Hepworth, M (1988) (also reference 18) *Age Conscious: An Illustrated Look at Age*

Prejudice, Age Concern Scotland, Edinburgh.

7 Mullen, C and von Zwanenberg, F (1988) *Out of the Twilight: A Resource Pack on Ageism in the Media,* BBC Education, London.

8 Age Concern England (1990) Age Discrimination: Responses to Questionnaire (unpublished), London.

9 Norman, A (1987) (also reference 17) *Aspects of Ageism: A Discussion Paper,* Centre for Policy on Ageing, London.

10 Power, B (1987) *Attitudes of Young People to Ageing and the Elderly,* National Council for the Aged, Dublin.

11 Lessing, D (1985) *The Diaries of Jane Somers,* Penguin Books, Harmondsworth.

12 Stevenson, O (1989) *Age and Vulnerability,* Edward Arnold/Age Concern England, London.

13 Midwinter, E and Tester, S (1987) *Polls Apart?: Older Votes and the 1987 General Election,* Centre for Policy on Ageing, London.

14 Macdonald, B with Rich, C (1985) (also reference 19) *Look Me in the Eye: Old Women, Ageing and Ageism,* The Women's Press, London.

15 Lehr, U (1987) The Elderly Patient in Medical Practice. In: *The Elderly Patient in General Practice,* edited by W Meier-Ruge, Karger, Basle.

16 Day, E (1986) Time to Value the Golden Age. *Nursing Times,* 15 October, London.

17 Norman, A (1987) (reference 9).

18 Hepworth, M (1988) (reference 6).

19 Macdonald, B with Rich, C (1985) (reference 14).

20 Cutler, S J (1985) Ageing and Attitudes about Sexual Morality. *Ageing and Society,* 5 (no 2), Cambridge, England.

21 Gilleard, C (1986) *UK Quizzes on Ageing,* Age Concern Scotland, Edinburgh.

22 Wells, N and Freer, C (1988) *The Ageing Population: Burden or Challenge?,* Macmillan, London.

23 King's Fund Centre (1989) *They Aren't in the Brief: Advertising People with Disabilities,* London.

3   NO SENSE OF URGENCY: AGE DISCRIMINATION IN HEALTH CARE

1 King's Fund (1988) (also reference 9) *Promoting Health Among Elderly People: A Statement from a Working Group,* King Edward's Hospital Fund for London.

2 Wilkin, D and Hughes, B (1986) The Elderly and the Health Services. In: *Ageing and Social Policy: A Critical Assessment,* edited by C Phillipson and A Walker, Gower, Aldershot.

3 Office of Population Censuses and Surveys (1989) *General Household Survey 1986,* HMSO, London.

4 Office of Population Censuses and Surveys (1988) *The Prevalence of Disability Among Adults,* HMSO, London.

5 Gallup (1988) (also reference 32) *Attitudes of the Elderly Towards Healthcare,* prepared for the MSD Foundation, London.

6 Health Advisory Service (1982) *The Rising Tide: Developing Services for Mental Illness in Old Age,* Sutton.

7 Beveridge, W (1942) *Social Insurance and Allied Services,* Cmd 6404, HMSO, London.

8 A Time to Die (1989). *The Economist,* 5 August, p 19, London.

9 King's Fund (1988) (reference 1).

10 Callahan, D (1986) (also reference 17) Health Care in the Aging Society: A Moral Dilemma. In: *Our Aging Society: Paradox and Promise,* edited by A Pifer and L Bronte, W W Norton, London.

11 Age Concern Institute of Gerontology (1988) *The Living Will: Consent to Treatment at the End of Life, a Working Party Report,* Age Concern Institute of Gerontology and Centre for Medical Law and Ethics, London.

12 Beardshaw, V (1988) *Last on the List: Community Services for People with Physical Disabilities.* Research Report No 3, King's Fund Institute, London.

13 Social Services Committee (1988) *Fifth Report on the Future of the NHS (Session 1987-88)*, para 217, HMSO, London.

14 Jennet, B and Buxton, M (1990) When is Treatment for Cancer Economically Justified? *Journal of the Royal Society of Medicine,* 83, 25-28, London.

15 Maynard, A (1988) What Can We Afford? Paper delivered at the 1988 MSD Foundation Symposium Review on *Health Care in Old Age: Choices in a Changing NHS,* November, London.
16 Weale, A (ed) (1988) *Cost and Choice in Health Care: The Ethical Dimension,* King Edward's Hospital Fund for London.
17 Callahan, D (1986) (reference 10).
18 Taylor, R C and Buckley, E G (eds) (1987) *Preventive Care of the Elderly: A Review of Current Developments,* Royal College of General Practioners, London.
19 British Medical Association (1986) *All Our Tomorrows: Growing Old in Britain,* report of the British Medical Association's Board of Science and Education, London.
20 Tulloch, A J et al (1979) cited in British Medical Association (1986) (reference 19).
21 Office of Health Economics (1990) *Osteoporosis and the Risk of Fracture, OHE,* London.
22 Royal College of Physicians (1989) (also reference 24) *Fractured Neck of Femur: Prevention and Management,* Royal College of Physicians of London.
23 Whitehead, M (1989) *Swimming Upstream: Trends and Prospects in Education for Health,* Research Report 5, King's Fund Institute, London.
24 Royal College of Physicians (1989) (reference 22).
25 Fletcher, A (1990) (also reference 26) Screening for Cancer of the Cervix in Elderly Women. *Lancet,* 335, 97-99, London.
26 Fletcher, A (1990) (reference 25).
27 Roberts, M (1989) Breast Screening: Time for a Re-think? *British Medical Journal,* London.
28 Fentiman, I S et al (1990) (also reference 29) Cancer in the Elderly: Why so Badly Treated? *Lancet,* April 28, pp 1020-1022, London.
29 Fentiman, I S et al (1990) (reference 28).
30 Department of Health (1989) *Working for Patients,* Cmd 555, HMSO, London.
31 Lewis, R R and McNab, W R (1990) The Future of Health Care for the Elderly. *Journal of the Royal Society of Medicine,* 83, 2-3, London.
32 Gallup (1988) (reference 5).
33 Royal College of Physicians of London and Royal College of Psychiatrists (1989) *Care of Elderly People with Mental Illness,* London.
34 Department of Health (1989) *Caring for People,* Cmd 849, HMSO, London.

4 THE BENEFITS OF OLD AGE? AGE DISCRIMINATION AND SOCIAL SECURITY

1 Walker, A (1980) (also references 3 and 21) The Social Creation of Poverty and Dependency in Old Age. *Journal of Social Policy,* 9, no 1, 49-75, Cambridge, England. Townsend, P (1986) Ageism and Social Policy. In: *Ageing and Social Policy: A Critical Assessment,* edited by C Phillipson and A Walker, Gower, Aldershot.
2 Department of Health and Social Security (1984) (also reference 13) *Pension Costs and Pensioners' Incomes,* HMSO, London.
3 Walker, A (1980) (reference 1). Walker, A (1981) Towards a Political Economy of Old Age. *Ageing and Society,* vol 1, pt 1, pp 73-94, Cambridge, England.
4 Taylor, F W (1947) *Scientific Management,* Harper, New York.
5 Graebner, W (1980) *A History of Retirement,* Yale University Press, New York.
6 Stead, F H (1920) *How Old Age Pensions Began to Be,* Methuen, London.
7 Thane, P (1982) *The Foundations of the Welfare State,* Longman, London.
8 Shragge, E (1984) *Pensions Policy in Britain,* Routledge, London.
9 Beveridge, W (1942) (also reference 33) *Social Insurance and Allied Services,* Cmd 6404, HMSO, London.
10 Booth, C (1989) *Pauperism, a Picture, and Endowment of Old Age, an Argument,* Macmillan, London.
11 Department of Social Security (1989) *Social Security Statistics 1989,* HMSO, London.
12 Townsend, P (1979) (also references 14, 27 and 32) *Poverty in the United Kingdom,*

Penguin Books, Harmondsworth.
13 Department of Health and Social Security (1984) (reference 2).
14 Townsend, P (1979) (reference 12). Mack, J and Lansley, S (1985) *Poor Britain*, Allen and Unwin, London.
15 Central Statistical Office (1990) *Social Trends 20*, HMSO, London.
16 Central Statistical Office (1985) *Social Trends 15*, HMSO, London. Central Statistical Office (1988) *Economic Trends 18*, HMSO, London.
17 Thomson, D (1984) The Decline of Social Welfare: Falling State Support for the Elderly Since Early Victorian Times. *Ageing and Society,* 4, 451-482, Cambridge, England.
18 Walker, R, Lawson, R and Townsend, P (1983) *Responses to Poverty,* Heinemann, London.
19 Chapman, K (1990) Looking Around Europe, *Eurolink Age Bulletin,* March, London.
20 Hedstrom, P and Ringen, S (1987) Age and Income in Contemporary Society; A Research Note. *Journal of Social Policy,* 16, 227-239, Cambridge, England.
21 Walker, A (1980) (reference 1).
22 Norman, A (1985) *Triple Jeopardy,* Centre for Policy on Ageing, London.
23 Walker, A (1987) The Poor Relation: Poverty Among Old Women. In: *Women and Poverty in Britain,* edited by C Glendinning and J Millar, Wheatsheaf, Brighton.
24 Walker, A (1986) (also reference 37) Pensions and the Production of Poverty in Old Age. In: *Ageing and Social Policy: A Critical Assessment,* edited by C Phillipson and A Walker, Gower, Aldershot.
25 Department of Social Security (1989)

Supplementary Benefit Take-up 1985/86: Technical Note, DSS, London.
26 Townsend, P (1981) Elderly People with Disabilities. In: *Disability in Britain,* edited by A Walker and P Townsend, Martin Robertson, Oxford.
27 Townsend, P (1979) (reference 12). Walker, A (1981) Disability and Income. In: *Disability in Britain,* edited by A Walker and P Townsend, Martin Robertson, Oxford.
28 Martin, J, Meltzer, H and Elliot, D (1988) (also reference 30) *The Prevalence of Disability Among Adults: Report 1,* HMSO, London.
29 Thompson, P with Buckle, J and Lavery M (1988) *Not the OPCS Survey,* Disability Income Group, London.
30 Martin, J, Meltzer, H and Elliot, D (1988) (reference 28).
31 Scott, N (1988) *Statement on the Publication of the First OPCS Report on Disability,* Department of Social Security, London.
32 Townsend, P (1979) (reference 12).
33 Beveridge, W (1942) (reference 9).
34 Department of Social Security (1990) (also reference 39) *The Way Ahead,* HMSO, London.
35 Disability Alliance (1987) *Poverty and Disability: Breaking the Link,* Disability Alliance, London.
36 Age Concern Scotland (1989) (also reference 38) *Shortchange,* Age Concern Scotland, Edinburgh.
37 Walker, A (1986) (reference 24).
38 Age Concern Scotland (1989) (reference 36).
39 Department of Social Security (1990) (reference 34).

5 A BAD BUSINESS: AGE DISCRIMINATION AND THE CONSUMER

1 Churchill, D (1989) (also reference 3) The rosy potential offered by 'greys'. *Financial Times,* 21 December, London.
2 Roberts, E (1972) *The Retired as Consumers,* manifesto series no 13, Age Concern England, London.
3 Churchiill, D (1989) (reference 1).
4 Batty, M (1989) (also reference 6) *Europe and the Mature Consumer,* an address to

the National Council of Women, March, London.
5 British Academy of Film and Television Arts (BAFTA) conference (1988) (also references 7 and 9) *Capturing the Grey Panther,* 21-22 September, London.
6 Batty, M (1989) (reference 4).
7 British Academy of Film and Television Arts (BAFTA) conference (1988)

(reference 5).
8 Gabriel, J (1989) *The Old Are Not Marketed To: A Paper for the Coming of Age,* Age Concern England, London.
9 British Academy of Film and Television Arts (BAFTA) conference (1988) (reference 5).
10 Age Concern England (1985) (also reference 15) *The Elderly Shopper: Report of a Working Party,* London.
11 Isaacs, B (1988) The Owlmark and the Thousand Elders *Geriatric Medicine,* November, Orpington.
12 Cold Shoulder for a Shining Example (1990). *Yours,* January, London.
13 Woolf, H (1983) *Older People in the Consumer Market Place,* Age Concern England conference, July, London.
14 Perlitz, M (1989) The Marketing Implications of the Ageing European Population. *European Business Journal,* March.

15 Age Concern England (1985) (reference 10).
16 Abrams, M (1985) *A Survey of the Older Shopper,* Age Concern England, London.
17 Office of Population Censuses and , Surveys (1989) *General Household Survey 1986,* HMSO, London.
18 National Institute for Social Work (1981) *At Home in a Boarding House: Report of an Independent Working Party for the Personal Social Services Council,* London.
19 National House Builders Council (1989) *The NHBC Sheltered Housing Code,* London.
20 Brown, D and Edwards, J (1989) *User-Friendly Products: A Discussion Paper for Age Concern England.* Research Institute for Consumer Affairs (RICA), London.
21 Association of Assistant Librarians (1989) Equal Opportunities: Ageism – a Policy Statement. *Journal of the Association of Assistant Librarians,* London.

6   DEFENDING THE RIGHT TO WORK: AGE DISCRIMINATION IN EMPLOYMENT

1 *Sunday Times,* 29 January 1989, London.
2 Phillipson, C (1982) *Capitalism and Construction of Old Age,* Macmillan, London.
3 *Employment Gazette,* 97, no 4, 170-171, HMSO, London.
4 Questions in Parliament (1984) *Employment Gazette,* 92, 31, HMSO, London.
5 House of Commons Employment Committee (Session 1988-89) *The Employment Patterns of the Over-50s,* vol 11 HMSO, London.
6 Wells, B (1989) (also reference 17) The Labour Market for Young and Older Workers. *Employment Gazette,* 96, 319-331, HMSO, London.
7 Memorandum submitted by the Department of Employment to House of Commons Employment Committee (Session 1988-1989), *The Employment Patterns of the Over-50s,* vol 11, p 93, HMSO, London.
8 Interview with Norman Fowler, The Future of Work. *The Guardian,* 22 December 1988, London.
9 Bosanquet, N (1987) *A Generation in*

Limbo, Public Policy Centre, London.
10 Training in Britain: Key Statistics (1988) *Employment Gazette,* 96, no 3, 130-143, HMSO, London.
11 *Training in Britain* (1989) HMSO, London.
12 Equal Opportunities Commission (1989) Age Discrimination: Over the Hill at 45? *Equal Opportunities Review 25,* May/June, London.
13 Naylor, P (1987) (also reference 29) In Praise of Older Workers. *Personnel Management,* November, pp 44-48, London.
14 Supplementary Memorandum submitted by the Department of Employment to House of Commons Employment Committee (Session 1988-89) *The Employment Patterns of the Over-50s, vol III* p 121, HMSO, London.
15 Doering, M, Rhodes, S and Schuster, M (1983) (also reference 18) *The Ageing Worker,* Sage Books, London.
16 Parker, S (1982) *Work and Retirement,* Allen and Unwin, London.
17 Wells, B (1989) (reference 6).
18 Doering, M, Rhodes, S and Schuster, M

(1983) (reference 15).
19 National Economic Development Office (1989) *Defusing the Demographic Timebomb,* London.
20 Jacobs, K and Rein, M (1986) *The Future of Early Retirement,* Working Paper Series, Science Centre, Berlin.
21 Memorandum submitted by the Department of Employment to House of Commons Employment Committee (Session 1988-89) *The Employment Patterns of the Over-50s,* vol 11, p 96, HMSO, London.
22 House of Commons, Third Report from Social Services Committee (Session 1981-82) *Age of Retirement,* HMSO, London.
23 Pletz, P (1990) *Older People – Appreciated Assets?* Paper to Fifth Annual Conference of the Association for Educational Gerontology, 26-28 March, Keele.

24 Pepper, C (1982) *Age Discrimination in Employment: A Growing Problem in America.* Select Committee on Aging, House of Representatives, Washington D.C.
25 Mackaronis, C (1986) The US Age Discrimination in Employment Act. *Ageing International,* Autumn/Winter, Washington D.C.
26 Casey, B and Bruche, G (1982) *Work or Retirement? Labour Market Policy for Older Workers in France, Britain, the Netherlands, Sweden and the USA,* Gower, Aldershot.
27 Laslett, P (1989) *A Fresh Map of Life,* Weidenfeld and Nicolson, London. Johnston, S and Phillipson, C (eds) (1986) *Education and Older Learners,* Bedford Square Press, London.
28 *Employment Gazette,* 97, no 6, 277, HMSO, London.
29 Naylor, P (1987) (reference 13).

7 YOUR COUNTRY DOESN'T NEED YOU!: AGE DISCRIMINATION AND VOLUNTARY SERVICE

1 Central Statistical Office (1990) *Social Trends,* HMSO, London.
2 Department of Health Circular HC (81) 15, HMSO, London.
3 Age Concern England (1989) Retirement Forum: Responses to Questionnaire (unpublished), London.

POSTSCRIPT: WHAT DO YOU THINK?

1 Age Concern England (1989) *Retirement Forum Responses to Questionnaire* (unpublished), London.
2 *Sex Discrimination: a guide to the Sex Discrimination Act* (1975), HMSO, London.
3 *Racial Discrimination: a guide to the Race Relations Act* (1976), HMSO, London.
4 Sheldon, J H (1948) *The Social Medicine of Old Age,* Oxford University Press, London.

About Age Concern

This is one of a wide range of publications produced by Age Concern England – National Council on Ageing. In addition, Age Concern England is actively engaged in training, information provision, research and campaigning for retired people and those who work with them. It is a registered charity dependent on public support for the continuation of its work.

Age Concern England links closely with Age Concern centres in Scotland, Wales and Northern Ireland to form a network of over 1,400 independent local UK groups. These groups, with the invaluable help of an estimated 250,000 volunteers, aim to improve the quality of life for older people and develop services appropriate to local needs and resources. These include advice and information, day care, visiting services, transport schemes, clubs, and specialist facilities for physically and mentally frail older people.

Age Concern England
Astral House
1268 London Road
London SW16 4EJ
Tel: 081 769 8000

Age Concern Scotland
54A Fountainbridge
Edinburgh EH3 9PT
Tel: 031-228 5656

Age Concern Wales
4th Floor
1 Cathedral Road
Cardiff CF1 9SD
Tel: 0222 371821/371566

Age Concern Northern Ireland
6 Lower Crescent
Belfast BT7 1NR
Tel: 0232 245729

PUBLICATIONS FROM AGE CONCERN

A wide range of titles is published under the Age Concern imprint.

PROFESSIONAL TITLES

CAN WE AFFORD OUR FUTURE?
Mike Reddin and Michael Pilch

A collection of radically different views on how to achieve the best kind of pension system to provide an adequate retirement income for everyone, now and in the future.
£4.95 0 86242 038 5

LIVING, LOVING AND AGEING
Sexual and personal relationships in later life
Wendy Greengross and Sally Greengross

Sexuality is often regarded as the preserve of the younger generation. At last, here is a book for older people and those who work with them which tackles the issues in a straightforward fashion, avoiding preconceptions and bias.
£4.95 0 86242 070 9

OLD AGE ABUSE
Mervyn Eastman

Old age abuse is an often neglected and overlooked phenomenon of our society. Very little has been recorded about the causes and consequences of physical abuse against old people. Now, for the first time, a series strictly based upon the author's 14 years of experience in the field of social services, presents the frustrating dilemma facing some of those who act in violence to those whom they may love, as well as the tragic consequences for the old person against whom the violence is directed.
£5.00 0 86242 030 x

THE LAW AND VULNERABLE ELDERLY PEOPLE
Edited by Sally Greengross

This report raises fundamental questions about the way society views and treats older people. The proposals put forward seek to enhance the self-determination and autonomy of vulnerable old people while ensuring that those who are physically or mentally frail are better protected in the future.
£6.50 0 86242 050 4

TAKING GOOD CARE
A handbook for care assistants
Jenyth Worsley

As the first book written specifically for care staff, this publication will quickly become the primary reference source for both public and private sectors. Produced in 'handbook' style it deliberately avoids jargon and technical terms and presents the information in a highly accessible format, illustrated with many case histories. Topics covered include the role of the assistant, the resident's viewpoint, activities and groupwork, and the latest research into the ageing process.
£6.95 0 86242 072 5

AGE CONCERN INSTITUTE OF GERONTOLOGY RESEARCH PAPER SERIES

COLLABORATION IN CARE
An Examination of Health and Social Service Provision for Mentally Frail Old People
ACIOG Research Paper No.2
Jenny Wright, Carolyn Ball and Peter Coleman

A comparison between two health districts in the South of England, exemplifying good practice but revealing the lack of contact, communication and feedback amongst professionals, and the repercussions this has for the elderly mentally infirm and their carers.
£5.00 0 86242 067 9

CREATING A BREAK
A Homecare Relief Scheme for Elderly People and their Supporters
ACIOG Research Paper No.3
Patricia Thornton

An in-depth examination of the scheme 'In Safe Hands', a project offering flexible and responsive relief care, which Age Concern York has been involved with since 1981.
£7.95 0 86242 069 5

DEMENTIA AND HOME CARE
A Research Report on a Home Support Scheme for Dementia Sufferers
ACIOG Research Paper No.4
Janet Askham and Catherine Thompson

This research paper examines and evaluates a major innovative homecare scheme co-ordinating services provided for dementia sufferers, and considers the challenge presented to planners and policy-makers
£12.95 0 86242 091 1

OLD AND ILL
Private Nursing Homes for Elderly People
ACIOG Research Paper No.1
Linda Challis and Helen Bartlett

A study of the private and voluntary nursing home industry, this systematic investigation discloses valuable information on the nature of homes, proprietors and consumers.
£10.00 0 86242 059 8

TITLES CO-PUBLISHED WITH EDWARD ARNOLD

THE 36-HOUR DAY
Caring at home for confused elderly people
Nancy L Mace and Peter Rabins MD
£7.50 0 34037 012 2

AGE AND VULNERABILITY
A guide to better care
Olive Stevenson
£6.95 0 34048 670 8

COUNSELLING OLDER PEOPLE
A creative response to ageing
Steve Scrutton
£8.95 0 34042 073 1

THE LIVING WILL
Consent to treatment at the end of life
A Working Party report
£3.95 0 34049 142 6

REHABILITATION OF ETHNIC MINORITY ELDERS
Edited by Mandy Squires
Published December 1990
(Price to be announced)

If you would like to order any of these titles, please write to the address below, enclosing a cheque or money order for the appropriate amount. Credit card orders may be made on 081-679 8000. A full publications catalogue is available on request.

Age Concern England (Dept ARD1)
FREEPOST
1268 London Road, London SW16 4EJ

INFORMATION FACTSHEETS

Age Concern England produces a series of 30 information factsheets, covering subjects such as income support for residential care, help with heating, television licence concessions and holidays. If you are working with or for older people, a subscription to the factsheet folder service entitles you to revised factsheets as they are updated through the year.

A monthly Information Circular is also produced, providing subscribers with a review of current developments in services and legislation as they affect older people. New publications and reports and relevant conferences and courses are also featured.

Further details available from the Information and Policy Department.

Age Concern England
Astral House
1268 London
London SW16 4EJ
Tel: 081-679 8000

INDEX